CHECKUPS, SHOTS AND ROBOTS

TRUE STORIES ABOUT HOW DOCTORS TREAT US

Written and illustrated by DAVID RICKERT

KANEPRESS

AN IMPRINT OF ASTRA BOOKS FOR YOUNG READERS

New York

Once more, to Jack and Lily

Kane Press
An imprint of Astra Books for Young Readers, a division of Astra Publishing House
astrapublishinghouse.com

Printed in Malaysia

ISBN: 978-1-6626-7017-6 (hc)
ISBN: 978-1-6626-7018-3 (eBook)

Library of Congress Cataloging-in-Publication Data

Names: Rickert, David, author.
Title: Check-ups, shots, and robots : true stories behind how doctors treat us / David Rickert.
Other titles: True stories behind how doctors treat us
Description: First edition. | New York : Kane Press, An imprint of Astra Books for Young Readers, [2024] | Audience: Ages 8-12 | Audience: Grades 4-6 | Summary: "Comic-format stories explore the origins and histories of medicine and medical breakthroughs from ancient herbal remedies to modern vaccines, with activities guiding readers in researching more medical history and how to draw comics"-- Provided by publisher.
Identifiers: LCCN 2024012814 (print) | LCCN 2024012815 (ebook) |
ISBN 9781662670176 (hardcover) | ISBN 9781662670183 (ebk)
Subjects: LCSH: Medical care--History--Juvenile literature. | Physicians--Juvenile literature.
| Medicine, Preventive--History--Juvenile literature. | Medical care--History--Comic books, strips, etc. | Physicians--Comic books, strips, etc. | Medicine, Preventive--Comic books, strips, etc.
Classification: LCC R130.5 .R53 2024 (print) | LCC R130.5 (ebook)
| DDC 610--dc23/eng/20240424
LC record available at https://lccn.loc.gov/2024012814
LC ebook record available at https://lccn.loc.gov/2024012815

First edition

10 9 8 7 6 5 4 3 2 1

The text is set in Gill Sans SemiBold.
The speech bubbles are set in Romper DB.
The titles are hand-lettered by David Rickert.
The illustrations for this book were created using Procreate on an iPad with finishing touches and cleanup done in Adobe Photoshop on a MacBook Pro.

Contents

INTRODUCTION: ERIC AND HIS APPENDIX

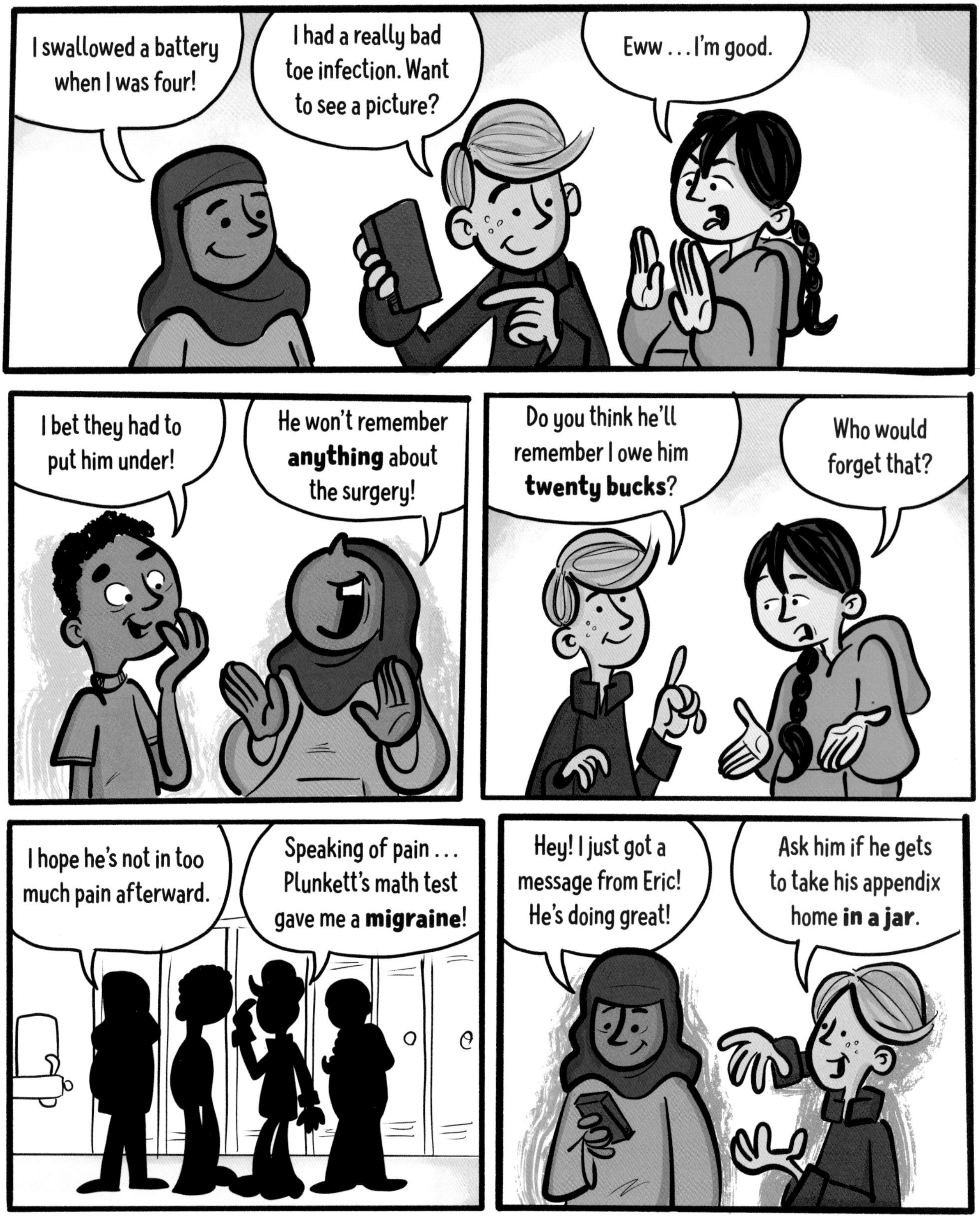
I swallowed a battery when I was four!
I had a really bad toe infection. Want to see a picture?
Eww . . . I'm good.
I bet they had to put him under!
He won't remember **anything** about the surgery!
Do you think he'll remember I owe him **twenty bucks**?
Who would forget that?
I hope he's not in too much pain afterward.
Speaking of pain . . . Plunkett's math test gave me a **migraine**!
Hey! I just got a message from Eric! He's doing great!
Ask him if he gets to take his appendix home **in a jar**.

CHECKUPS OR WHY DO I HAVE TO GO TO THE DOCTOR? I'M NOT SICK!

I can't believe I have to go to the doctor today. I'm feeling great!

You might feel great, but . . .

Haven't you heard about the **intestinal spider**?

Uh . . . no?

It crawls into your mouth while you're sleeping and creeps down to your belly!

Once it's there it lays a bunch of eggs.

Big eggs?

No. Very small. But when they hatch, millions of spiders crawl out of your butt!

Waaugh!

LATER . . .

There's **no such thing** as an intestinal spider. She was just messing with you.

Whew! What a relief!

But have you heard of the **nostril beetle**?

CHAPTER 1:

EARLY CHECKUPS

A sudden illness.
A mysterious pain.
A routine checkup.

People have visited a doctor for thousands of years for these same reasons. Doctors and other caregivers long ago didn't have our tools or a lot of medical knowledge, but they still came up with ways to figure out what was wrong with a patient.

A **giant beaver** attacked me!

During prehistoric times, if you weren't feeling well, you might have been treated by **your mother**!

What she knew had been passed down from previous generations, and she knew **a lot**.

This won't hurt a bit.

She would probably have treated you with herbs, but exactly which ones and how people used them remain a mystery.

For a long time, religion and medicine were closely tied. If you were injured in

ANCIENT EGYPT (3100–332 BCE)

you'd be fixed up by a **priest-physician.**

The Egyptians believed that good health not only came from proper care, but also from your relationship with other people, animals, and the universe. (So basically, everything else besides you.)

I'm at one with nature.

They were resourceful people who knew how to use what was around them to treat health problems.
And a lot of their treatments can be found in your kitchen today!

onions (skin rashes)

garlic (fatigue)

cloves (colds)

curry (purification)

prunes (inflammation)

yeast (stomach issues)

Do **not** try these at home!

You are **not** a priest-physician.

They also knew how to dress wounds. They used raw meat to stop bleeding,

added honey to avoid infections,

and bound wounds with linen bandages, which were changed often.

Ancient Chinese doctors, over 3,000 years ago, knew a lot about how to diagnose and treat illness. Just like doctors today, they started by taking your pulse. However, these doctors spent **over an hour** taking the pulse of a patient to determine how healthy they were. And they recorded their findings in poetic language:

These doctors also examined poop as an indicator of possible illness.

firmness

color

amount

And they looked at **tongues**—their size, shape, color, and flexibility—to learn about their patients' overall health. If there was a coating on it, that meant digestive problems.

So how did Chinese doctors treat illness? One method they used was

ACUPUNCTURE

In acupuncture thin needles are gently inserted into your skin at specific places on your body.

Don't worry! The needles are **tiny**, so you don't feel them!

Doctors believed acupuncture worked by helping the energy flow in your body. In traditional Chinese medicine, this energy is called *qi* (pronounced "chee").

These Chinese doctors were onto something, because acupuncture is still used today. People get it to help with headaches or backaches, or just to relieve tension and stress. **Tiny needles** can lead to **big results**!

When the energy flowed smoothly, you felt healthy and happy. But if the energy got stuck or blocked, you might feel not so good. Acupuncture helped to unblock the energy and make it flow freely again.

If you lived in ancient Greece in the 400s BCE, you might have been lucky to have a guy named

HIPPOCRATES

as your doctor. In fact, you'd be lucky to have him **today**!

Hippocrates was a great listener and observer. He believed you could tell a lot about what was wrong with people from a thorough examination. You'll recognize these things he did as part of your checkups too!

checking pulse

checking breathing

checking temperature

Hippocrates was also keen on the close examination of bodily fluids, just like the Chinese doctors. **Really close!**

tasting urine

looking at earwax

smelling poop

inspecting vomit

All of this may seem like a lot of disgusting work, but Hippocrates believed that bodily fluids were the best way to find if anything was wrong with you.

So what **was** wrong with you, according to Hippocrates? He combined the work of many ancient philosophers and developed the theory of

THE FOUR HUMORS!

This may sound funny, but it was serious business, and was how people determined what was wrong with you for centuries. The **four humors** theory spread throughout Europe and China and India.

Hippocrates believed that the four humors were four basic bodily fluids. If you had a balance of the humors in your body, you'd feel in tiptop shape. Too much of any of them threw your body out of whack and caused all illness and disease.

Therefore, by examining bodily fluids, and which ones might be in excess, you could tell what was wrong and where the imbalance was.

Hippocrates deserves credit for being one of the first people to link illness to problems with the body and not supernatural causes.

Too much PHLEGM (brain) leads to trouble breathing, stomach issues, low energy

Too much BLOOD (heart) leads to fevers, inflammation, mood swings

Too much BLACK BILE (spleen) leads to skin problems, depression, insomnia

Too much YELLOW BILE (liver) leads to joint pain, poor eyesight, anger issues

So what caused an imbalance of the humors? Things like:

CHAPTER 2: MEDICINE GOES TO SCHOOL!

Lots of civilizations had the same idea as Hippocrates, and over the next several centuries, all around Europe, Africa, Asia, and the Middle East, apprenticeships allowed students to learn from established physicians.

However, the first **modern** medical school was established in the 9th century in Salerno, Italy. For centuries, no other school came close to having better doctors and textbooks.

Any important school needs a fancy name, and this one was called the Schola Medica Salernitana.

THE Schola Medica Salernitana

One of the superstar teachers at the school was

CONSTANTINE THE AFRICAN

In the 11th century, he brought a vast collection of medical knowledge to the school—mostly his translations of the great masters of Arabic medicine.

> If only I could carry this library on a small handheld device!

SALERNO

And the collection just grew from there as scholars from various countries added to the stores of knowledge.

By the 13th century, the schola had become the most important source of medical knowledge in western Europe.

Much of the medical wisdom gathered there continued to be used for the next several centuries.

And a lot of those smart people were **women**!

You might think that it was unusual for women to be doctors back then, and you'd be right. But these women doctors, called

THE WOMEN OF SALERNO

One of these women, named **TROTA**, is widely considered to be the first **gynecologist** (a doctor that specializes in women's medicine).

knew that many physicians, especially men, had a lack of understanding of women's health issues.

One day while studying at the schola . . .

Ugh! Men don't know **anything** about women's health.

No kidding!

Women need doctors to help with **pregnancy**!

And to take care of **newborns**!

There's just no easy way for physicians to find that information!

I **know**! Let's write a **book**!

And so they began to study and write.

Trota and the women of Salerno spent countless hours to bring together the best knowledge from Arab medical texts about good medical practices for women. They wrote about . . .

Their work appears in three books called the *Trotula*. They were the only books available about women's health issues and male physicians learned **a lot**!

Trota and the other woman taught physicians important skills for taking care of women who were about to be mothers and helped prevent deaths during childbirth.

CHAPTER 3: MODERN MEDICINE

A few centuries later, in the early American colonies, people lacked established schools like the Schola Medica Salernitana.

But before too long—in the 1700s to be exact—physicians from Europe came over and began to practice medicine.

And these physicians also wanted medical schools. The first one, the College of Philadelphia, opened in 1765. Over the next few decades, medical schools opened at Columbia, Harvard, and Dartmouth. Students now had a place to learn medical practices from overseas.

One doctor named

WiLLiAM OSLeR

is often called the father of modern medicine. Not only was he one of the founding professors of the Johns Hopkins Hospital in 1893, but he transformed the relationship between doctors and students.

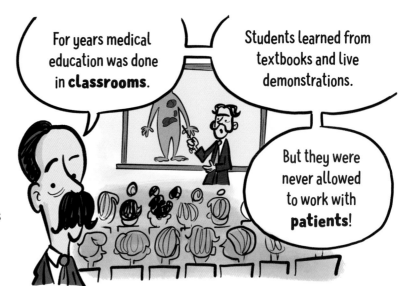

For years medical education was done in **classrooms**.

Students learned from textbooks and live demonstrations.

But they were never allowed to work with **patients**!

I thought, *Why not give students some hands-on experience?*

I let my students come with me as I examined my patients.

These students were given the opportunity to diagnose the patient under my supervision.

If they were wrong, I could correct them.

Broken leg? . . . No . . . Rabies? . . . I don't think so . . . Mosquito bites?

14

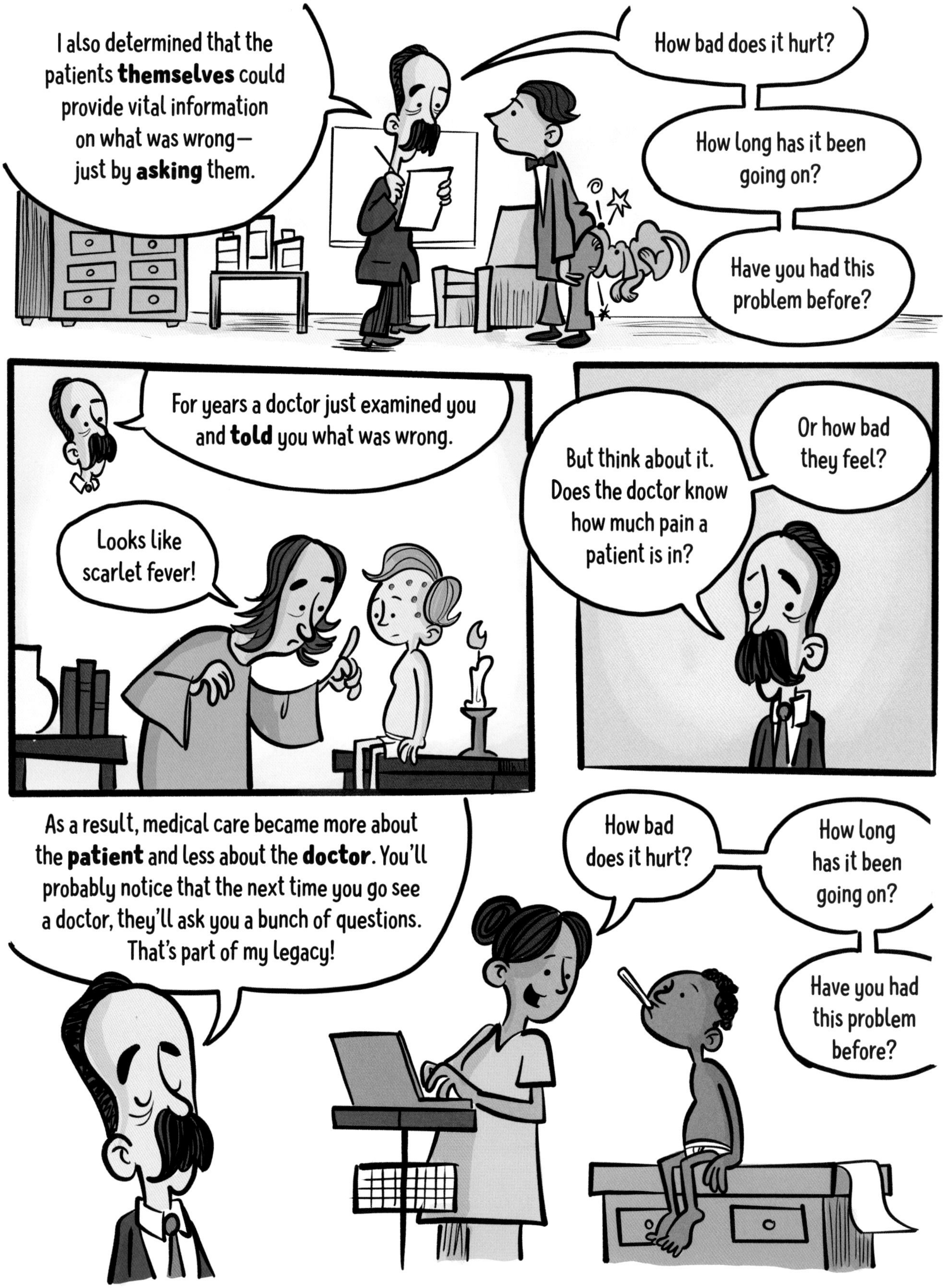

I also determined that the patients **themselves** could provide vital information on what was wrong— just by **asking** them.
How bad does it hurt?
How long has it been going on?
Have you had this problem before?
For years a doctor just examined you and **told** you what was wrong.
Looks like scarlet fever!
But think about it. Does the doctor know how much pain a patient is in?
Or how bad they feel?
As a result, medical care became more about the **patient** and less about the **doctor**. You'll probably notice that the next time you go see a doctor, they'll ask you a bunch of questions. That's part of my legacy!
How bad does it hurt?
How long has it been going on?
Have you had this problem before?

Throughout history there have always been doctors who have truly wanted to help anybody that needed medical treatment. Another 19th-century doctor was an extraordinary woman:

REBECCA LEE CRUMPLER

I fell off **my horse.**

After the Civil War, many formerly enslaved people had trouble getting medical care.

Many of them lacked the money to get to a doctor and pay for treatment.

Also, some doctors refused to treat Black people! Even though slavery was abolished, prejudice was still alive and well.

But I wanted to make sure that **everyone** had access to **good medical care!**

Crumpler had already done something that no one else had done: in 1864, she became the first Black woman to earn a medical degree (and she was one of the few women to do so).

And for a time, she practiced medicine in Boston.

But once the Civil War ended, Crumpler felt a calling.

I'll treat **everyone** who needs medical care, regardless of whether they are Black or white.

Or if they can pay!

She moved to Richmond, Virginia, where a lot of formerly enslaved people lived.

Through the generous help of charities and missionary groups, she and other Black doctors were able to provide free care for the over 30,000 Black people living in Richmond who needed it.

However, not everyone was on board with what Crumpler was doing. During her time in Richmond other doctors gave her a hard time.

A **woman** can't be a doctor!

Leave medicine to **men**!

Yeah! **White men!**

And why would you want to treat **former slaves**?

They can't pay!

Because former slaves are people too.

People who need access to good medical care!

It took **more than a century** for her accomplishments to be recognized. No one knew where she was buried until a group of doctors and historians found the plot and raised money for a gravestone. And now her house is part of the Boston Women's Heritage Trail!

THE CHECKUP

When you visit the doctor for your annual visit, they will perform a series of tests that will measure whether or not your body is working properly. Some of them will seem familiar from what you've read so far. But **what** do these tests measure?

Check temperature to detect infection early

Check hearing and vision (do you need glasses or hearing aids?)

Measure blood pressure to make sure your heart is working correctly

Listen to your heart, lungs, and gut for any irregularities that might be of concern

Test reflexes to see if your brain is properly connected to your muscles

Measure your height and weight to see if you are growing OK

Press your belly to see if any organs are enlarged or painful

WHAT'S NEXT: IMPLANTABLE CHIPS

Scientists are working on implantable chips called **motes** that doctors can place at various points in your body to measure your health. **Don't worry!** They are too small to be seen by the naked eye.

I'm going to be **part robot!**

These motes could eventually detect problems with your heart, lungs, blood, and other parts of the body before you even notice a problem. The mote would then communicate by ultrasound to an external device to register the problem.

Alert! A problem detected!

Right now, these motes can't do much more than monitor your temperature. But scientists are hopeful that soon they will be able to detect more serious problems, like cancer or heart attacks, so that they can be treated early before they become too serious.

DISEASES AND INFECTIONS OR I HAVE A FEVER AND I CAN'T STOP COUGHING!

21

CHAPTER 4:
GERMS are EVERYWHERE!

Germs are tiny creatures that you can't see, but they can make you feel pretty crummy.

THEY ARE everywhere!

In the air...

Ugh...

...on your skin...

Ecch!

...and even on the food you eat!

Urp!

Don't worry! There are some nasty germs that cause real problems. But many germs are perfectly harmless, and in some cases help our bodies to work normally.

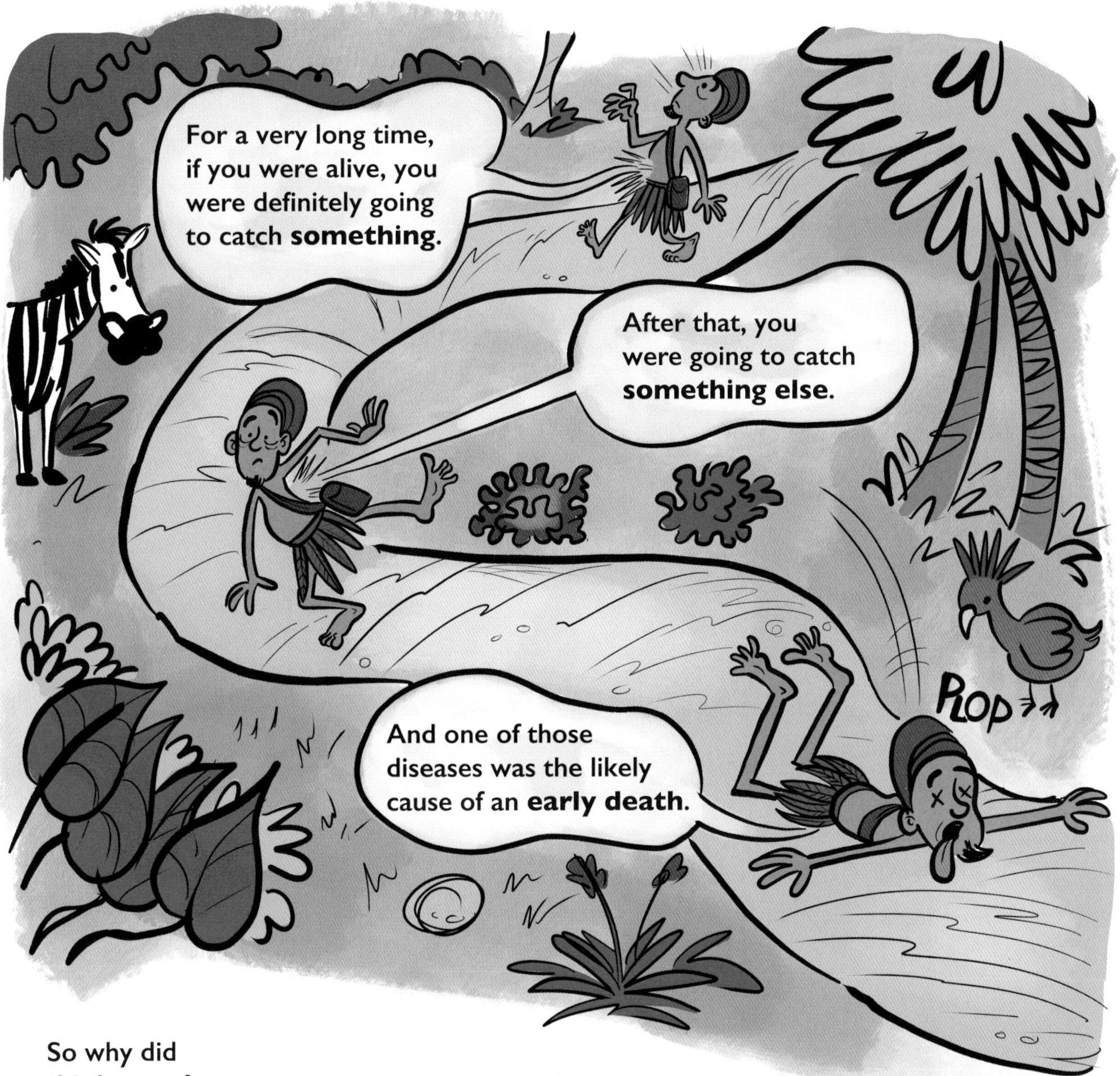
For a very long time, if you were alive, you were definitely going to catch **something**.
After that, you were going to catch **something else**.
PLOP
And one of those diseases was the likely cause of an **early death**.

So why did this happen?

It wasn't just because for a long time people didn't have the medicines we have today.

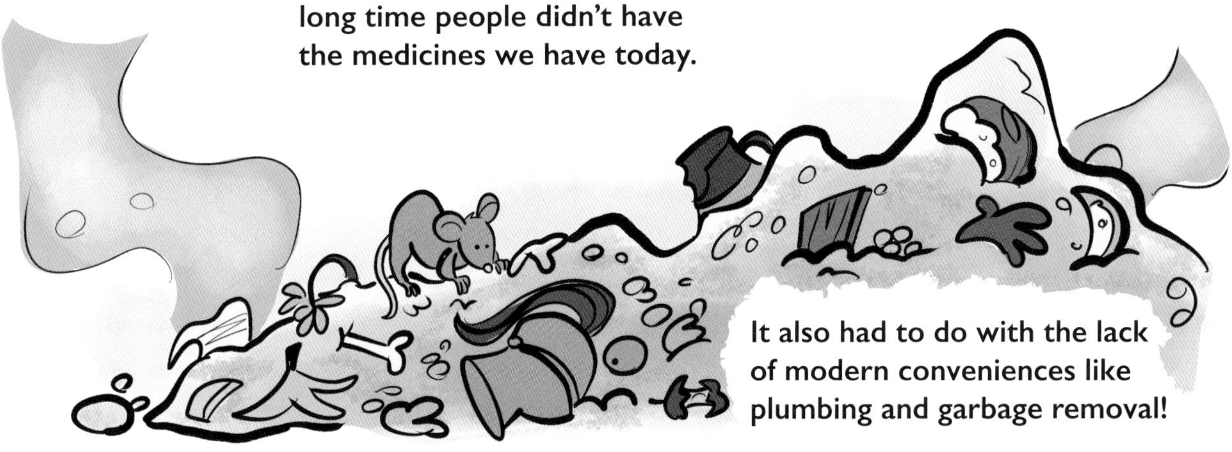

It also had to do with the lack of modern conveniences like plumbing and garbage removal!

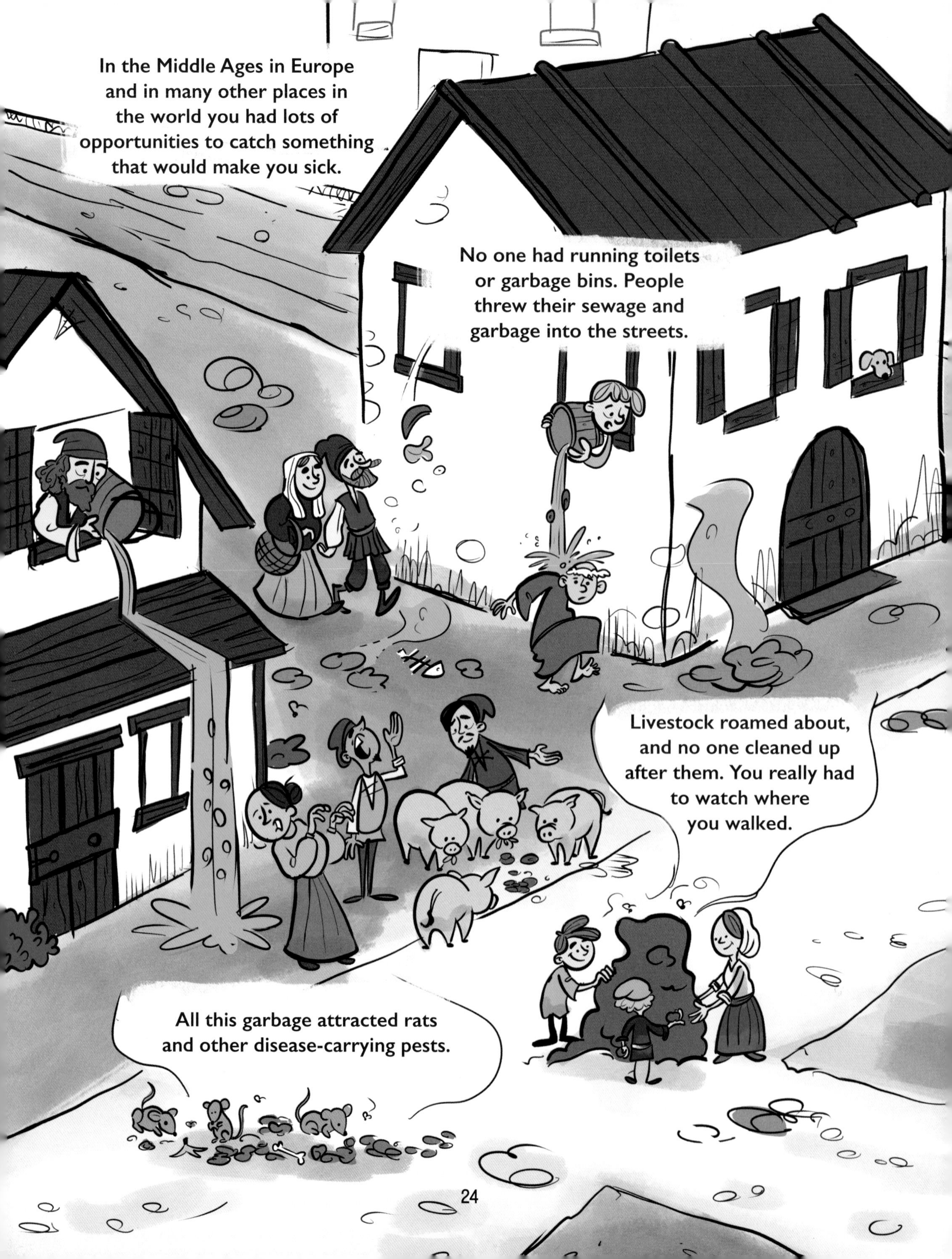
In the Middle Ages in Europe and in many other places in the world you had lots of opportunities to catch something that would make you sick.
No one had running toilets or garbage bins. People threw their sewage and garbage into the streets.
Livestock roamed about, and no one cleaned up after them. You really had to watch where you walked.
All this garbage attracted rats and other disease-carrying pests.

People also threw their garbage and sewage into rivers, which poisoned the water supply. If you were brave enough to drink the water, you were drinking old, rotten food and poop and urine.

Butchers and tanners added cast-off animal parts.

Plus, it all smelled **awful!**

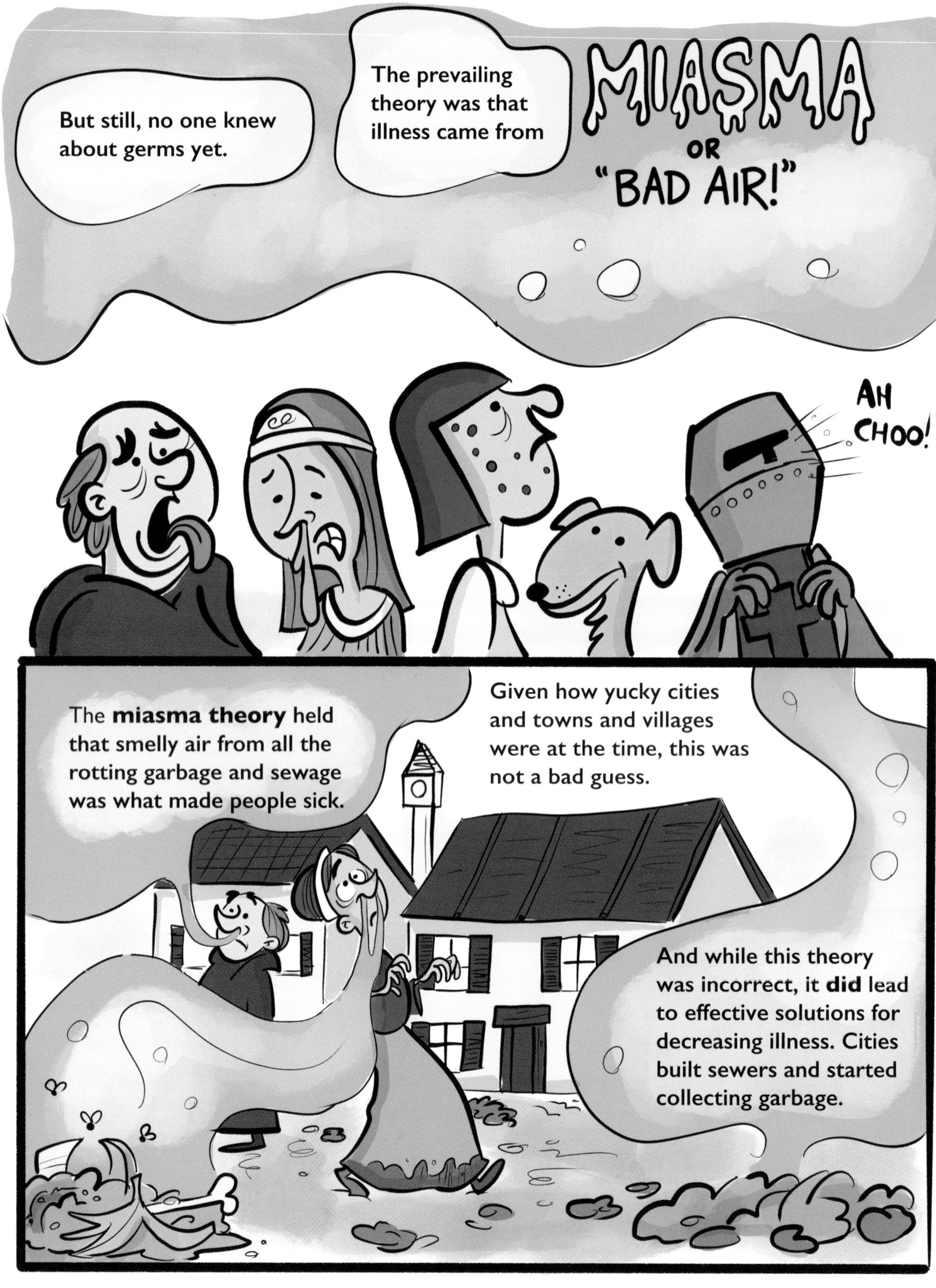
But still, no one knew about germs yet.
The prevailing theory was that illness came from
MIASMA
OR
"BAD AIR!"
AH CHOO!
The **miasma theory** held that smelly air from all the rotting garbage and sewage was what made people sick.
Given how yucky cities and towns and villages were at the time, this was not a bad guess.
And while this theory was incorrect, it **did** lead to effective solutions for decreasing illness. Cities built sewers and started collecting garbage.

Some scientists questioned miasma theory. They thought something else must be responsible for making people sick, and they tried to figure out what it was.

They finally started to figure out what was going on when they began to use an amazing invention: THE MICROSCOPE!

The first microscopes, developed around 1590, gave scientists a closer look at everything.

And as microscopes improved, scientists could start to see things that were invisible to the naked eye.

Well I'll be!

And after a few centuries of research, what they saw led them to believe that disease didn't come from miasma, but instead from the tiny world they had discovered.

One Dutch guy in particular loved to look through microscopes. In fact, he made his own! And they could magnify clearly up to **250 times**! His name was

ANTON VAN LEEUWENHOEK

and in the 1670s he was one of the first people to discover the amazing world of tiny creatures we can't see with our eyes.

Leeuwenhoek's microscope

And through careful study he made a groundbreaking discovery . . .

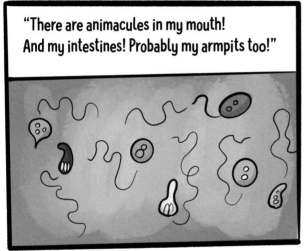

Think about how mind-blowing this must have been. A whole world of cells and microorganisms that no one knew existed. But it took a few more centuries before scientists were able to prove that these tiny living things could be responsible for diseases. Here are a couple of smart fellows that figured that out.

LOUIS PASTEUR

Why does **some** wine spoil and some wine **doesn't**?

And how can we prevent it from happening?

In the mid-1800s in France, another microscope nut named **Louis Pasteur** loved to study microorganisms. He was also a good problem solver. He set out to solve a mystery.

Spoilage was a problem with other beverages, such as milk. And of course, foods could go rotten as well. But Pasteur, armed with his trusty microscope, figured out the truth.

Aha! **Bacteria** are the real culprit!

How did these bacteria get into the wine? Some people thought that they came from the wine itself—that bacteria were the result of **spoilage** and not the **cause**.

Hogwash!

In 1859 Pasteur conducted an experiment—this time with beef broth and some weirdly shaped glass flasks.

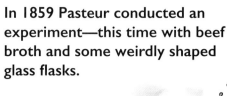

He discovered that the broth didn't spoil if he kept dust, microbes, and other particles from falling into it—even if it was exposed to air.

air can get in

microbes get trapped

broth stays good!

As a result, Pasteur developed what is called **germ theory**.

Bacteria cause infections and contamination! And not the other way around!

But what should we do about it?

?

Pasteur's inventive method was to heat milk and other liquids briefly to 60-100 degrees Celsius to kill off any bacteria.

You have to wait until **after** she's milked!

By helping reduce the risk of spoiled food, pasteurization saved millions of lives, and continues to do so today!

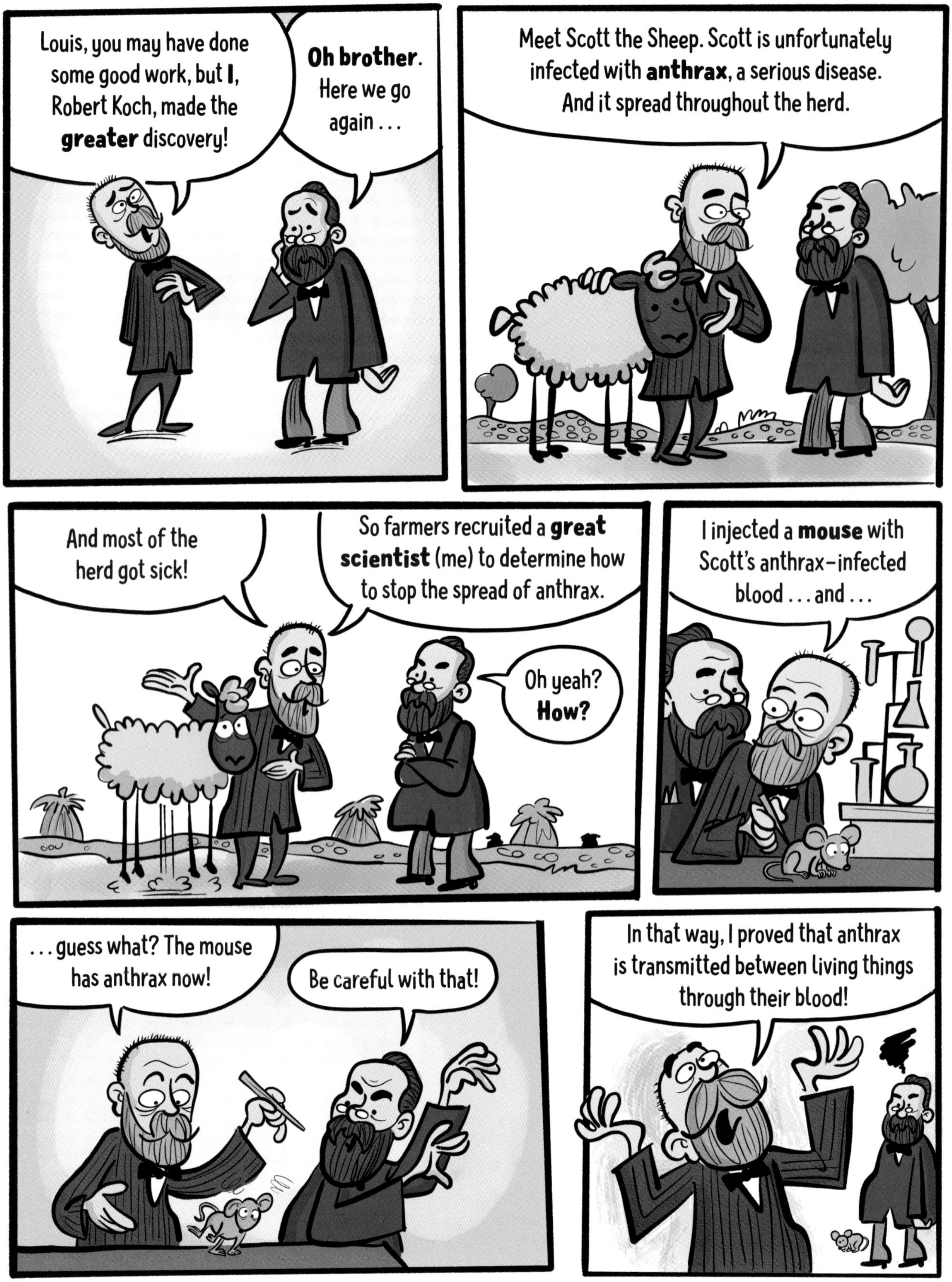
Louis, you may have done some good work, but **I**, Robert Koch, made the **greater** discovery!
Oh brother. Here we go again . . .
Meet Scott the Sheep. Scott is unfortunately infected with **anthrax**, a serious disease. And it spread throughout the herd.
And most of the herd got sick!
So farmers recruited a **great scientist** (me) to determine how to stop the spread of anthrax.
Oh yeah? **How?**
I injected a **mouse** with Scott's anthrax-infected blood . . . and . . .
. . . guess what? The mouse has anthrax now!
Be careful with that!
In that way, I proved that anthrax is transmitted between living things through their blood!

And for the first time, a specific microorganism was linked to a particular disease.

Are you done yet?

Not even close! I also studied **tuberculosis**—a deadly disease—and discovered what caused it.

And developed a **vaccine** for it!

I developed vaccines **too**—for **your** anthrax! And rabies and cholera! But that's in the next section!

OK, then . . . I'll just polish my Nobel Prize . . . which I won for my work with tuberculosis. Do **you** have one of these?

You know I don't! I died six years before they started giving them out!

Robert—let's declare a truce.

We both did great work proving that bacteria cause infection in people.

Agreed. We both saved millions of lives. And millions of sheep!

Now that people knew about germs, you would think that medical care would improve. Not so! Infection continued to be a problem in what might seem to be an unlikely place:

HOSPITALS!

HOSPITALS

For many years, hospitals were pretty gross. In fact, you had a better chance of surviving if you **didn't** go to one.

Unwashed hands and tools from one patient to the next

poop, pee, and vomit

poor air circulation

sheets not changed for days

One doctor by the name of

JOSEPH LISTER

decided to tackle the problem.

A raging fever! Hot skin! Swelling! Disgusting discharge!

And by worse I mean **dead**!

I bet **germs** are causing the infections. I think I have a solution!

Instead of getting **better** after surgery my patients are getting **worse**!

I bet I can find something that will kill bacteria.

And our patients will live!

Lister used a special liquid called **carbolic acid** that killed germs. He cleaned wounds . . .

. . . and sterilized instruments.

SQUIRT SQUIRT

And he made sure the operating room was clean as well.

SQUIRT SQUIRT

Lister's goal was to prevent infection before it happened with clean instruments and hands. And a sterile hospital environment.

No more **blood and puke!** Clean it up!

My method **worked!** The number of people getting sick after surgery went **way down**,

and they recovered faster too.

Doctors still use Lister's antiseptic techniques to keep surgeries clean and infection-free.

Finally! Scientists had discovered what made people sick. Soon, they got to work on developing drugs that would fight infection in the body, known as **antibiotics**. And a scientist found one of the most effective ones completely by **accident**!

One day in 1928, in a lab at St. Mary's Hospital in London, **Alexander Fleming**, a scientist studying bacteria, returned from vacation. He discovered that he had left out a dish of colonies of *Staphylococcus* bacteria (which causes serious skin infections) by mistake. And he saw something **fascinating**!

While he was gone, mold had snuck into the lab, finding a nice home in the bacteria and killing it.

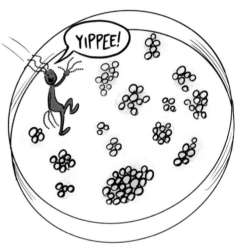

Most people would have just thrown the dish out and started over. **But not Fleming**! He decided to take a closer look.

Could this be the solution to the problem of infection?

Fleming took some samples of the mold and was able to get the same effects of the mold on bacteria. He called it **penicillin** (because the mold was a member of the *Penicillium* genus).

TAKE THAT!

36

PENICILLIN

However, making penicillin in large amounts was tough. It took Fleming and his team **several** years to figure out how to manufacture it.

Penicillin was rushed overseas to action in World War II, where it saved the lives of countless soldiers.

But through trial and error, other determined scientists discovered methods to mass-produce penicillin. In 1942, US drug companies only developed enough to treat 10 people. By 1945, they produced **6,852 billion doses**.

Before penicillin, even the smallest cut or scrape could be deadly because of the risk of infection. But penicillin became the most widely used antibiotic because it did a great job fighting off infection. Today if you get an infection and have to see a doctor, there's a good chance a dose of penicillin will do the trick!

CHAPTER 6
How ANTIBIOTICS WORK

You might start out with one tiny bacterial cell in your body. But bacteria want to take over the whole system! One bacterium can quickly divide into two. And two divide into four, four divide into eight, and before too long you're feeling **really lousy!**

But antibiotics get your system back in order by:

Killing the bacteria . . .

BANG.

. . . or slowing their growth.

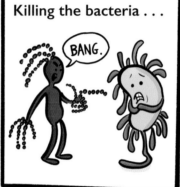

Why don't I take antibiotics for everything?

Colds and flus are caused by viruses, so antibiotics won't help. If you have a bacterial infection, like strep throat, antibiotics will help you get better.

Some illnesses aren't bacterial. Some can be caused by viruses. Bacteria can live outside the body. Viruses are smaller, and need a host, like one of your cells.

See ya, viruses! I'm going to the **throat!**

I don't care WHAT I have! I just want to get rid of it!

However, for all the good that antibiotics do, there's a serious problem:

ANTIBIOTIC RESISTANCE.

And according to many health organizations, it's one of our biggest health problems today.

Antibiotic resistance happens when bacteria adapt to antibiotics so they no longer work.

We become **superbugs**!

You'll never stop us then! We'll take over **the world**!

CAUSES OF ANTIBIOTIC RESISTANCE:

Taking too many antibiotics or taking them when they aren't needed

Antibiotics used in animals enter the environment through poop and urine.

Scientists warn that by 2050 over 10 million people will die from superbugs, and that even small infections will once again be potentially life-threatening.

Do your **worst**! I'm not afraid!

BUT THERE'S HOPE!!

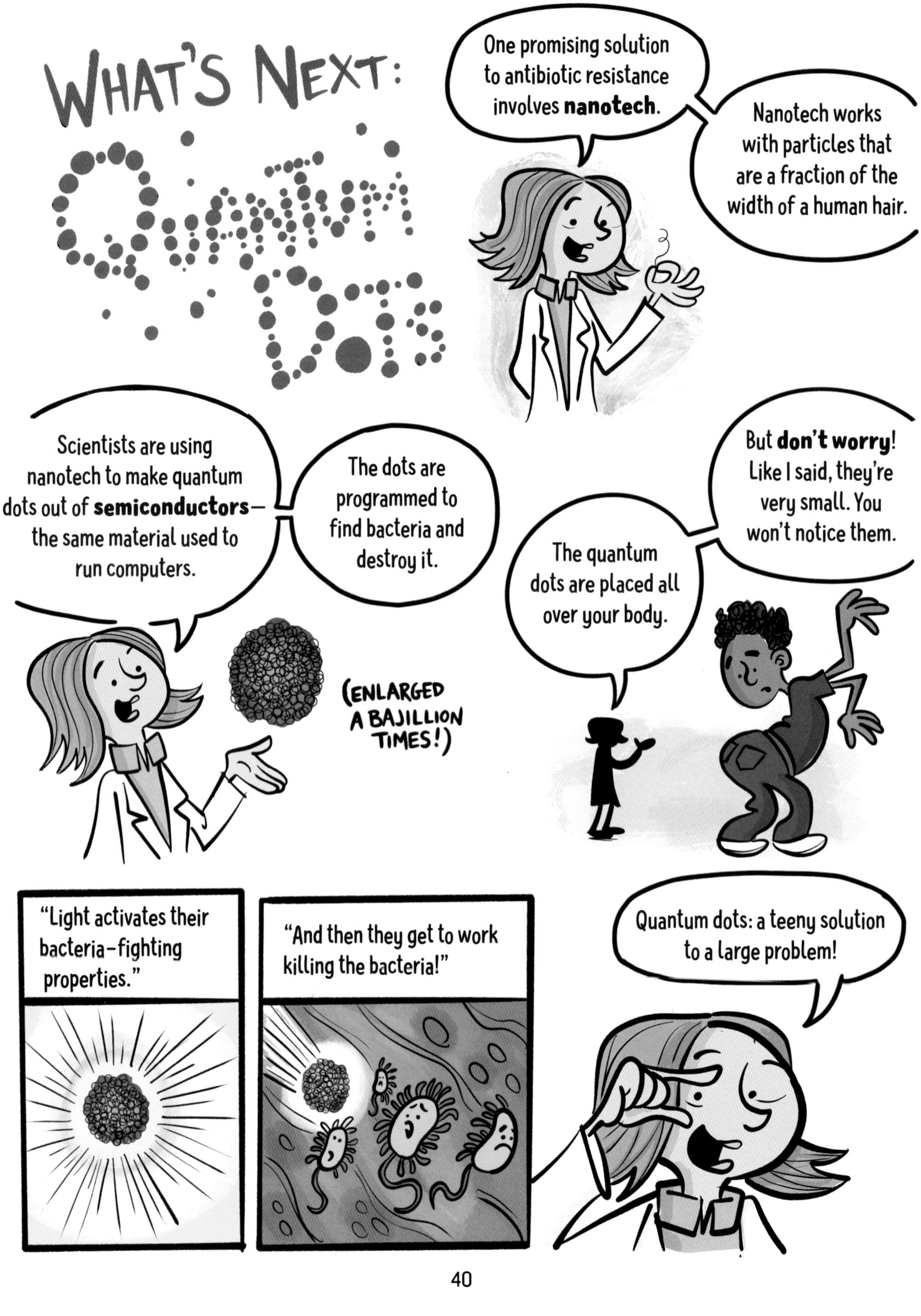

WHAT'S NEXT: QUANTUM DOTS
One promising solution to antibiotic resistance involves **nanotech**.
Nanotech works with particles that are a fraction of the width of a human hair.
Scientists are using nanotech to make quantum dots out of **semiconductors**—the same material used to run computers.
The dots are programmed to find bacteria and destroy it.
(ENLARGED A BAJILLION TIMES!)
The quantum dots are placed all over your body.
But **don't worry**! Like I said, they're very small. You won't notice them.
"Light activates their bacteria-fighting properties."
"And then they get to work killing the bacteria!"
Quantum dots: a teeny solution to a large problem!

VACCINES OR WHY DO I HAVE TO GET A SHOT?

CHAPTER 7: THE DISCOVERY of VACCINES

Centuries ago, North America was a pretty nice place to live. There was plenty of fresh air, and it was very quiet.

But it wasn't paradise. Many substances that could cause death or serious illness lurked in the air and water.

However, Native Americans of the time figured out a way to develop resistance to some pesky substances.

If something caused an allergic reaction, they found that eating small amounts of it would prevent this.

I started eating (ugh) **poison oak** every day!

I don't get rashes anymore!

I'm going to be immune to **broccoli**!

This method worked for allergies, but not for diseases, and especially not for a deadly one— **smallpox**.

For a long time, smallpox hadn't existed in North America. But explorers and traders brought it with them from Europe. Many Europeans had some immunity to it.

But the Native Americans did not. It wiped out 90 percent of the native population.

And it wasn't deadly for just them. Smallpox had been a huge problem everywhere for centuries.

One in three people who got it died. And it was almost always fatal for infants.

Smallpox often caused an **epidemic**— when a disease infects large numbers of people.

Smallpox enters the body through your lungs. At first you don't feel too bad.

Hah! I'm going to be **fine**!

But after two weeks, you develop a fever and fatigue, and then running sores and scabs. These are highly infectious!

Maybe not...

And this might lead to severe paralysis or, in many cases, death.

Around 1000 CE, people in China noticed that some people who had smallpox and lived never caught it again.

As a result of this startling discovery, they developed a simple vaccination technique called **variolation**.

Variolation involved giving people a little bit of smallpox so their bodies would learn how to fight it.

And in many cases, it **did** prevent serious cases of smallpox!

grind up infected scabs

rub them in a scratch in the skin or...

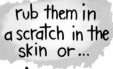

...blow them up the nostrils

Fast forward to 18th-century Europe, where smallpox was killing around **400,000 people every year**. And no one had a solution yet.

THAT IS UNTIL LADY MARY WORTLEY MONTAGU!

In 1717, Lady Mary Wortley Montagu traveled from England to Constantinople with her ambassador husband and her son.

While she was there, she noticed doctors using variolation to prevent smallpox.

I grow weary of this wretched smallpox!

I shall arrange for my son's treatment by these physicians.

Back in England, she and other doctors tested variolation on volunteers.

This method proves effective!

Success! Variolation worked!

Contaminating an individual with an ailment to avert the very ailment?

Preposterous! But it does bear fruit!

Once it was proven effective, variolation against smallpox became standard in England. Lady Montagu's solution was a lifesaver!

From our journey, I learned of a technique that saved numerous lives!

Smallpox was a problem in the English colonies as well. In 1721, a smallpox epidemic spread quickly through the colony of Massachusetts, infecting half of the people and killing 850.

But an enslaved person named

ONESIMUS

knew what to do!

Onesimus knew about variolation from living in Africa before he was enslaved and brought to Massachusetts. He taught the method to his enslaver, Cotton Mather.

Mather, along with his doctor and city officials, convinced 242 townspeople to try it out.

CLANG CLANG

HEAL THYSELF

Come and partake in measures that shall ward off affliction!

Gradually they saw that variolation was working! People who received it got less sick and had a better chance of surviving. It helped slow the spread of the disease, too.

And it was all thanks to Onesimus and his technique.

Your name shall echo throughout history!

I GOT SCABBED

In 2016, Onesimus was named one of the **greatest Bostonians** of all time.

But it was thanks to some **cows** that people got rid of smallpox for good.

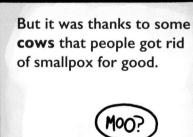

MOO?

Variolation was effective, but doctors were still looking for better methods.

In the mid-1700s in rural England, a country physician named Edward Jenner learned an interesting fact from a milkmaid.

People exposed to **cowpox** never get **smallpox**!

Cowpox is an infection carried by cows (hence the name). Farmers who worked with livestock might catch it. But it didn't make them as sick as smallpox did.

Jenner had an idea.

I'm going to treat **my son** with an infection of cowpox!

Then I'll see if he can catch smallpox.

Given what people knew about smallpox at the time, this was risky. But in the name of science, Jenner went forward confidently with his plan.

He took a small sliver of wood and tried to infect his son with cowpox.

Here goes nothing!

Jenner's son never got smallpox. The experiment was a success!

Whew!

But Jenner knew he needed more evidence. He tried the same experiment on James Phipps, the nine-year-old son of his gardener.

This time Jenner infected young James with cowpox, and then exposed him to smallpox several times.

But you never get sick!

I'm sick of you **infecting** me!

Jenner had created the **world's**

FIRST VACCINE!

Some people claim I have saved more lives than any other man.

Over time several more scientists built upon Jenner's vaccine, and health organizations distributed it around the globe.

In 1980, the World Health Organization declared that smallpox had been completely eradicated. It's the only disease that has been **completely destroyed**!

And the word "vaccine" comes from Jenner's work!

The word for "cow" in Latin is *vacca*!

HOLD ON!

This all might seem a little . . . weird. Let's stop for a second and think about what Jenner was doing.

WAS THIS OK?

Why not?

It turned out well, but was it OK to infect a child with a disease just to see if a risky procedure would work?

I might have **died**!

Plus, what did **I** get out of it?

Unfortunately, at the time it was common for doctors to try out cures on children, enslaved people, and prisoners— people who couldn't say no.

Often these people didn't know the risks involved or why they were being treated.

I promised prisoners they could get out of jail if I tested variolation on them!

They might have died, but after all, they were just **prisoners**!

Today we have **ethical guidelines** for testing potential procedures on patients.

Patients or their parents have to give consent and be fully aware of what they are getting into and the risks involved.

There has to be an **apparent benefit** to the patient while **minimizing risks**.

No one wants to end a life by being careless with vaccine research!

Chapter Eight

OTHER EPIDEMICS

Vaccines took a huge step forward in the 19th century, especially once doctors had accepted the idea of germ theory.

In fact, our friend Louis Pasteur developed the next two vaccines.

A cholera vaccine for chickens . . .

and a rabies vaccine for humans!

There were other deadly diseases that caused epidemics. And in some cases, people had to figure out how to stop the spread of the disease before they did anything else.

One was

YELLOW FEVER!

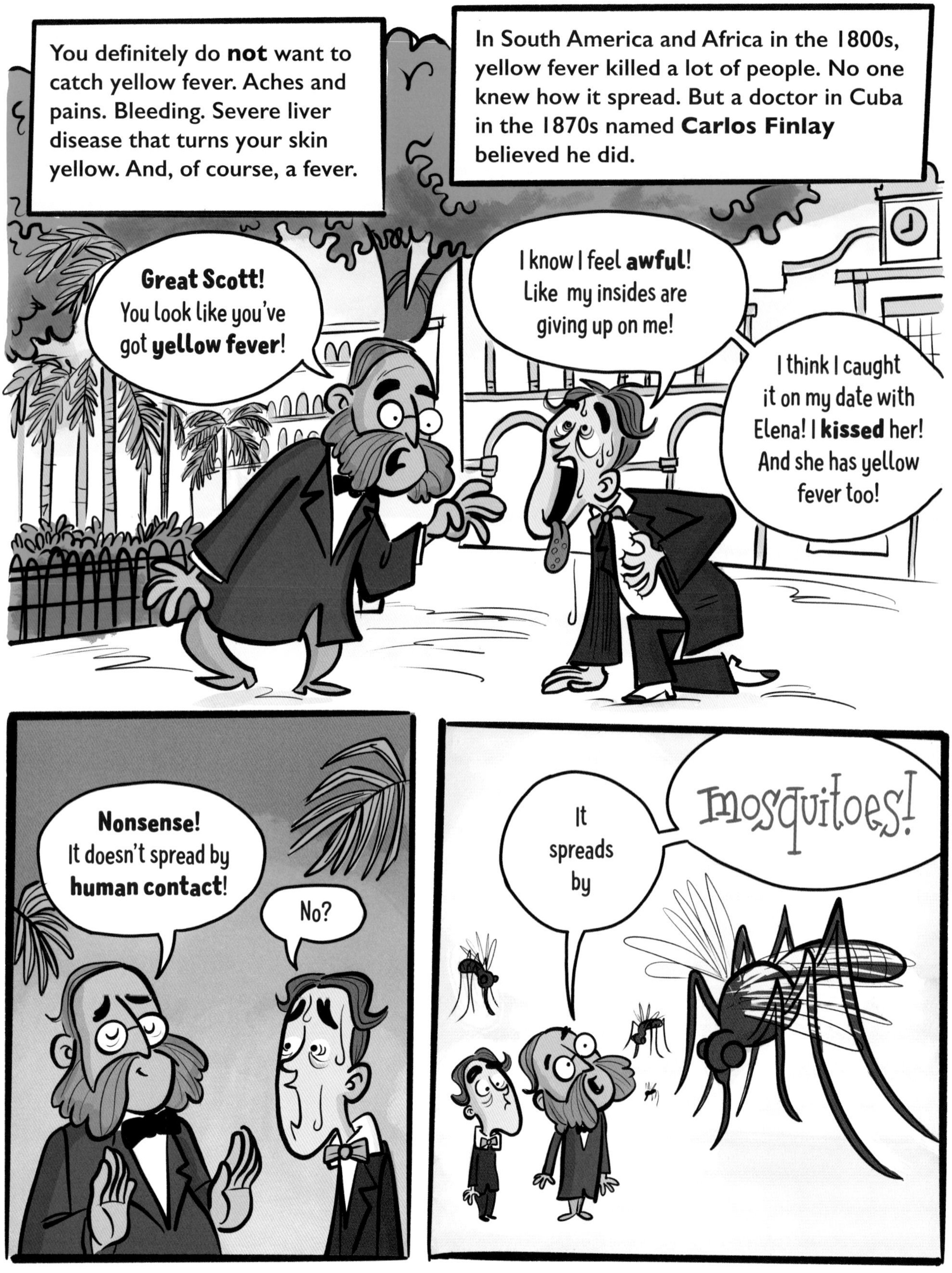
You definitely do **not** want to catch yellow fever. Aches and pains. Bleeding. Severe liver disease that turns your skin yellow. And, of course, a fever.
In South America and Africa in the 1800s, yellow fever killed a lot of people. No one knew how it spread. But a doctor in Cuba in the 1870s named **Carlos Finlay** believed he did.
Great Scott! You look like you've got **yellow fever**!
I know I feel **awful**! Like my insides are giving up on me!
I think I caught it on my date with Elena! I **kissed** her! And she has yellow fever too!
Nonsense! It doesn't spread by **human contact**!
No?
It spreads by
Mosquitoes!

But Finlay was correct! In 1900, the US Army Yellow Fever Commission proved Finlay's theory with their own batch of mosquitoes.

Therefore, the Cubans took measures to keep mosquitoes at bay.

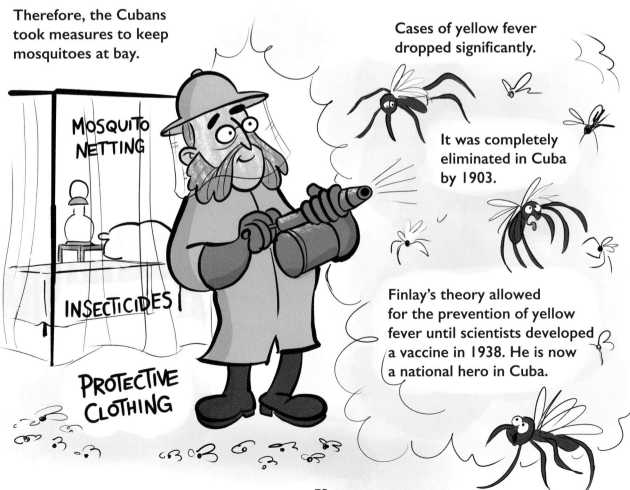

Cases of yellow fever dropped significantly.

It was completely eliminated in Cuba by 1903.

Finlay's theory allowed for the prevention of yellow fever until scientists developed a vaccine in 1938. He is now a national hero in Cuba.

THE NEXT KILLER DISEASE WAS:

Polio

How serious was polio? Polio is **highly contagious**. It causes paralysis for some and death for others. Children were the most likely to catch it.

A polio outbreak in New York City during the summer of 1916 killed 2,243 people and paralyzed more than 9,300 others (mostly kids under the age of ten). And it continued to be a deadly killer **every year thereafter**.

In 1952, almost **60,000 children** were infected in the US. **Thousands** were paralyzed. **More than 3,000** died.

Parents took desperate measures.

We stopped taking them to swimming pools and movie theaters! Too dangerous!

I wouldn't let my son play with new friends! Too risky!

Ever since the start of the polio epidemic, scientists had tried to find a cure but had no success.

The government stepped in.

In 1938, President Roosevelt (who was paralyzed from polio) established the National Foundation for Infantile Paralysis (or NFIP) to provide funding toward finding a cure.

Their famous campaign, called the March of Dimes, encouraged people to donate dimes to support research and development for a vaccine.

THE RACE TO FIND

One determined scientist by the name of **Jonas Salk** started to look for a vaccine in 1947. It took him **seven years** to find it.

Ha! I have it! (Not **polio**. The **vaccine**!)

In 1952, he developed a harmless version of polio that would teach the body's immune system to fight it.

I'm going to get to the bottom of this, you **nasty creatures**!

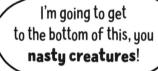

He studied the disease for a few years to see how it affected the body and how it spread.

THE POLIO VACCINE

Finally, on April 12, 1955 . . .

Success! Let's give it to **everyone**! And send it overseas!

Doctors started giving people the vaccine. By 1957, annual cases dropped from 58,000 to 5,600, and by 1961, only 161 people still had it.

In 1954, Salk and his team led one of the largest vaccine trials in history. Nearly 2 million children were part of the study.

This won't hurt a bit!

We (pant, pant) **did it!**

Once again, people could go to swimming pools and movie theaters without fear. All thanks to Jonas Salk and his smart and hardworking team!

COVID

Smallpox, yellow fever, and polio. All devasting diseases that caused a lot of alarm among people. And as you now know, new deadly viruses can still pop up without warning, like **COVID** in 2019.

Fortunately, we have learned a lot about how to prevent the spread of disease over time. Here are some things that helped during COVID that had also worked in the past!

Isolation and Quarantine: During plagues in the Middle Ages, people who were sick or suspected of being sick were often isolated from the healthy population for 40 days.

Travel Restrictions: In the 14th century, the city of Venice isolated the crew of incoming ships on islands for a time before coming ashore.

Hygiene Measures: During the cholera epidemics of the 19th century, doctors told people to wash their hands.

Mask Wearing: During the 1918 flu pandemic, people were advised or required to wear masks in public places.

Vaccination: Successful vaccines of the past made people less likely to get seriously ill and less likely to die.

Social Distancing: During the Ebola outbreaks in Africa, public gatherings were prohibited.

Public Health Campaigns: In the late 19th century, tuberculosis campaigns told people to cover their coughs and sneezes.

CHAPTER 9

VACCINES

Your vaccination journey begins before you can remember! Here are all the shots you've already had.

A few days old: Hepatitis B vaccine.

This protects from potentially dangerous infection.

Two months: first set of DTaP, Hib, PCV, and IPV vaccines.

These will help the immune system grow strong.

First birthday: MMR vaccine.

This shot will protect from measles, mumps, and rubella.

Preschooler: booster shots for DTaP, MMR, and Varicella.

These will help you stay healthy as you begin school.

And as new illnesses pop up, the scientific community continues to keep us healthy by developing new vaccines.

HOW DO VACCINES WORK?

Vaccines usually consist of **a dead or weakened** form of the bacteria or virus. Therefore, you won't get sick, but your body still thinks it might.

Once the vaccine is in your body, your immune system reacts by creating antibodies to work with existing cells to fight it.

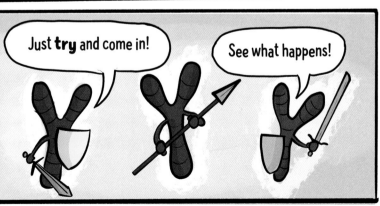

The antibodies remember how to fight the disease and remain in your system ready to fight off an infection if it does happen.

WHAT'S NEXT: EDIBLE VACCINES

In the future you might be able to get vaccines by doing something you already do: **eating fruits and vegetables**!

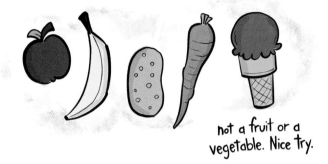

not a fruit or a vegetable. Nice try.

Biotechnologists (people who use technology to solve medical issues) have found a way to teach foods like potatoes, bananas, and corn how to manufacture vaccines while they grow.

All you'd need to do to be vaccinated is eat one of those foods.

But biotechnologists aren't doing this just because the vaccine tastes good. It will help prevent infections in countries where access to vaccines is scarce.

Today's vaccines are expensive to make and have to be refrigerated to be transported over long distances.

Edible vaccines will be cheaper to manufacture and easier to transport or grow where they are needed.

In the future, eating your fruits and veggies might have even **more** benefits!

VACCINES

VACCINES

PAIN or I HAVE A MONSTER HEADACHE!

CHAPTER 10:
ANCIENT PAIN RELIEF

Nobody enjoys pain. Since the dawn of humanity, to ease a stubbed toe or nagging sore throat, people have come up with ways to cope with pain.

Early humans relied on the resources around them, and learned which herbs could help with pain.

But people in early cultures didn't really understand pain.

In many cases they could figure out what was causing the pain.

I know what's wrong!

But what about pain **inside** the body? Or pain that just wouldn't go away? This perplexed them.

It's probably due to **evil spirits**!

But ancient civilizations found ways to fight pain by using what was nearby.

ANCIENT GREECE

We mixed **opium** from poppies with food or drink.

NATIVE AMERICANS

We chewed on **willow bark** for general aches and pains.

ANCIENT CHINA

Mint and menthol were used to soothe sore muscles and joints!

ANCIENT INDIA

Licorice and ginger helped with stomach issues.

AND MANY OF THESE REMEDIES ARE STILL USED TODAY!

Ancient civilizations had other solutions to pain that didn't involve herbs. They developed physical and mental techniques that are still used by doctors and therapists.

Ancient civilizations created cold compresses by soaking rags in cold water. If you lived in colder climates, ice or snow would do the trick.

And heat worked too! Ancient Romans developed **steam rooms** and **hot baths** to soothe their aches and pains.

And many ancient cultures learned that you could ease pain just by using your mind. In ancient India, doctors taught patients to **meditate**, which helped the mind ignore pain.

Breathing techniques directed energy to where the body needed healing, and chanting fostered a sense of peace.

The strangest pain relief from ancient times might shock you. **Literally!** And it doesn't involve a plant. It involves an animal!

THE NILE CATFISH

The Nile catfish produces an electric current, like an electric eel. Around 4700 years ago Egyptians fished them out of the Nile to treat pain.

A physician placed a catfish on the painful area. The Egyptians believed the electric shock helped with pain and started the healing process.

Did it actually work? No one knows for sure. But in the quest for pain relief, everything was worth a shot!

CHAPTER 11: Chemical painkillers

Early pain remedies could only do so much. They were fine if you had a headache, but not so great for surgery.

With no pain relief, surgery was difficult. The patient had to be restrained—the doctor couldn't operate while they were writhing around in pain.

And doctors had to work quickly or else risk prolonging the agony. Many people died from the shock of surgery.

For centuries, opium provided doctors with a natural pain remedy derived from poppies. However, no one was quite sure how much of it to give.

In the 16th century, **laudanum**—a solution of alcohol and opium with some spices added for flavor—came in controlled dosages that were easy to transport and administer.

It tasted better, too.

Laudanum allowed doctors in Europe to treat a variety of ailments like chronic pain, while also easing the pain of surgery.

It helped with diarrhea too!

However, there's one BIG problem with medications made from OPIUM.

Opium is **highly addictive**. In the 1800s, doctors realized how harmful opium was and restricted its use.

Even today, opioid addiction is a problem. Doctors carefully prescribe opioids so that patients don't develop a drug habit.

A more promising solution came in the form of **inhalants**—pain relief you breathed in. Inhalants not only numbed the pain, but also knocked people out while doctors operated.

And all it took was a couple scientists to see the possibilities for their use.

One day in 1844 a dentist named **Horace Wells** attended a live demonstration of the effects of **nitrous oxide**, or "laughing gas."

Wells saw a man under the influence of nitrous oxide laughing uncontrollably, even though he had just slammed his knee into a chair!

A curious Wells went back to his office and gave himself a dose of laughing gas.

His colleague did so and . . .

Wells revealed his findings to a former partner, dental surgeon **William Thomas Green Morton**.

Let's pull a tooth **in public**!

Then everyone will know what laughing gas can do!

A few months later, Wells stood in front of a group of Harvard medical students with a tray full of instruments and a patient full of laughing gas.

He started pulling on the bad tooth but . . .

Ouch! Stop!

Wells had not given enough laughing gas!

There was laughing, all right . . . from the crowd.

What a joke!

How humiliating!

Morton recognized the potential of Wells's discovery but thought **ether**, another inhalant, would work better than laughing gas. He spent two years learning how to properly administer ether.

On October 16, 1846, Morton stood before a group of medical students from Massachusetts General Hospital. A patient with a painful jaw tumor sat before him.

Morton used a device to cover the patient's mouth to administer the ether. The patient was soon unconscious.

During the next twenty-five minutes, surgeon John Collins Warren removed the tumor from the pain-free patient, who remained still and asleep.

The patient woke up. The surgery was a success.

I didn't feel **a thing**!

Historians have called Morton's use of ether and this surgery one of the most important events in human history. Pain-free surgery was now possible.

Patients no longer had to be restrained while enduring unimaginable pain, and doctors could take their time performing an operation carefully.

Surgeons could remove tumors without pain and trauma. They became brave enough to make minor repairs to the heart and the lungs. Surgical knowledge grew in leaps and bounds.

They were now able to perform intricate surgeries deep inside the body.

Within three months of this operation, ether anesthesia was being used around the world.

And this led to the development of other inhalants, like **chloroform**, which weren't exactly less dangerous, but easier to dose properly.

None of us will need surgery every day, but we **will** have the occasional bump or bruise that might require milder pain relief.

Something like

You might remember willow bark was a common pain reliever long ago.

People didn't know **why** it worked. Just that it did.

The secret ingredient was **salicin**, and in the 1800s chemists learned how to make it from scratch.

However, it tasted awful and caused stomachaches. (Sorry, buddy!)

In 1897, Felix Hoffman (**that's me**) figured out how to make a milder version of salicin while working for the Bayer Pharmaceutical Company in Germany.

It's about time!

The Bayer company named the new product "aspirin," manufactured it as pills, and sent it to pharmacies.

Today, aspirin is the world's most widely used over-the-counter medication.

74

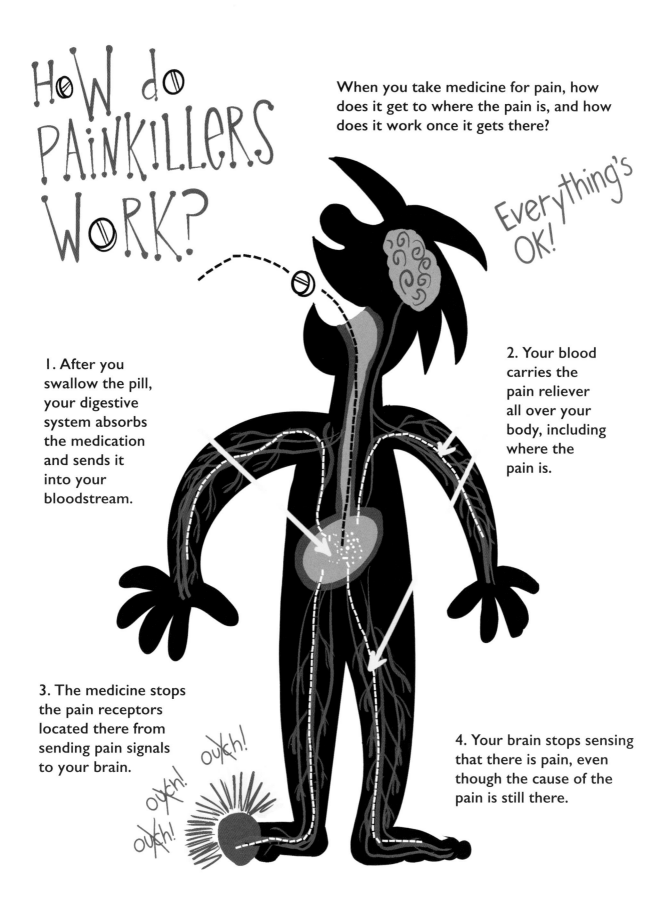

HOW DO PAINKILLERS WORK?

When you take medicine for pain, how does it get to where the pain is, and how does it work once it gets there?

Everything's OK!

1. After you swallow the pill, your digestive system absorbs the medication and sends it into your bloodstream.

2. Your blood carries the pain reliever all over your body, including where the pain is.

3. The medicine stops the pain receptors located there from sending pain signals to your brain.

4. Your brain stops sensing that there is pain, even though the cause of the pain is still there.

WHAT'S NEXT: VIRTUAL REALITY

There's a new solution to pain relief which blends ancient techniques with new technology.

You might know that **virtual reality** (or **VR**) is a technology that makes you feel like you are in another world.

You put on a VR headset—a set of goggles that gives you a 360-degree view of a virtual environment.

BREATHE DEEPLY...

In the virtual world the patient is in a peaceful, natural setting. It calms down the nervous system and helps focus attention away from the pain.

Some VR also has narration, so that the patient focuses on their breathing and directs their attention away from pain such as during cancer treatment or after surgery.

Researchers are hoping that VR will eventually help patients manage chronic pain through regular treatments.

76

SURGERY OR I BROKE MY LEG SKATEBOARDING!

Chapter 12:
EARLY
SURGERY

One of the earliest known (and most common) surgeries dates back more than 17,000 years to the Neolithic age. And it wasn't to fix broken toes. Or remove warts. It was

BRAIN SURGERY!

This is Kronk. He lives in what is now the Middle East. While out hunting, a woolly mammoth clubbed him on the head with his tusk. He needs medical help **quick**!

To solve this problem, Kronk's friend Skor drills a hole into the top of his skull to relieve the swelling. This procedure is called **trepanning**.

Kronk lives to hunt again. And he keeps the skull piece as a memento.

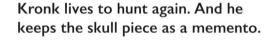

This won't hurt a bit!

Stop and think about this for a minute. Skor has no knowledge of anatomy or how the brain works.

Yet here he is, confidently making holes in skulls. And trepanation had a high success rate. Many people survived!

Having someone put a hole in your head is nobody's idea of a good time, so it must have been used only for serious problems like brain seizures or hemorrhages.

And what's really cool is that many cultures discovered trepanning at the same time. Trepanned skulls have been found in Europe, Asia, and South America—almost everywhere people lived.

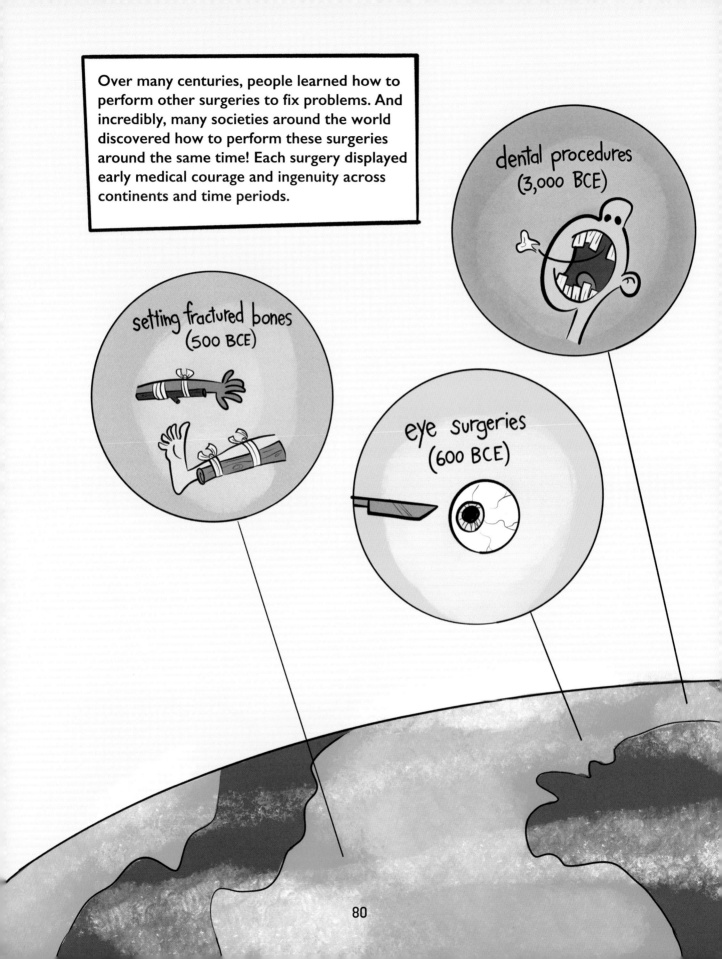

Over many centuries, people learned how to perform other surgeries to fix problems. And incredibly, many societies around the world discovered how to perform these surgeries around the same time! Each surgery displayed early medical courage and ingenuity across continents and time periods.

dental procedures
(3,000 BCE)

setting fractured bones
(500 BCE)

eye surgeries
(600 BCE)

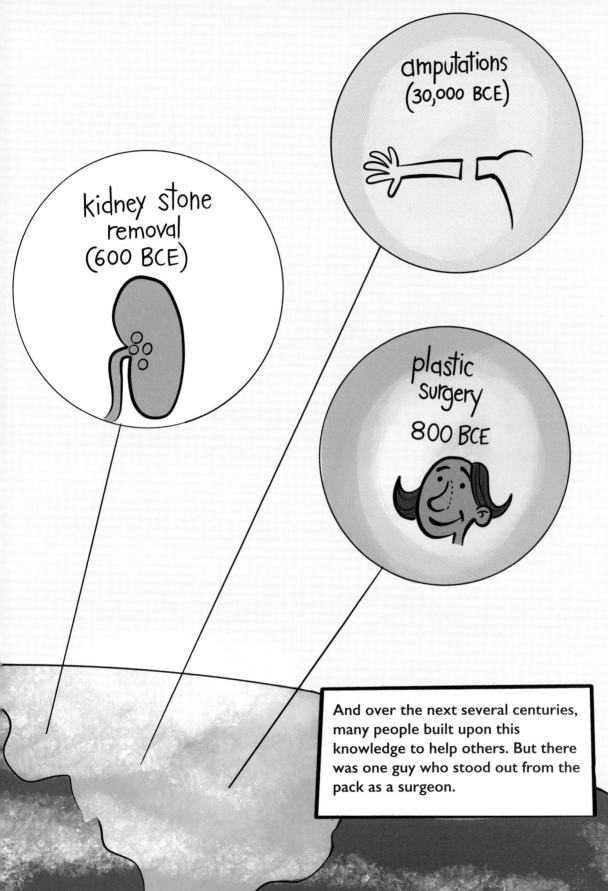

kidney stone removal (600 BCE)

amputations (30,000 BCE)

plastic surgery 800 BCE

And over the next several centuries, many people built upon this knowledge to help others. But there was one guy who stood out from the pack as a surgeon.

ABU AL-QASIM AL-ZAHRAWI

If you had a medical problem in Cordoba (the capital of Muslim Spain) during the 900s CE, al-Zahrawi was your guy. He knew how to fix just about everything.

I don't feel well. I've got all sorts of problems.

Good grief! Cataracts in your eyes!

An abscess in your liver!

Swollen tonsils!

And you appear to have a small bug stuck in your ear!

Huh? What did you say?

And who knows what else?

But I'll have you fixed up in no time!

There's a tool for every job!

Fortunately, al-Zahrawi had already pioneered many groundbreaking surgeries and invented close to 200 surgical instruments.

Al-Zahrawi pioneered many medical procedures. That's why he is another guy some people call the father of modern medicine!

Al-Zahrawi also wrote down almost **50 years'** worth of medical knowledge in a 30-volume set of books entitled *Al Tasreef Liman 'Ajaz 'Aan Al-Taleef.*

tracheotomies!

breast cancer surgery!

dislocated shoulder fixes!

childbirth!

urology!

syringes!

forceps!

His book was used in European countries for many centuries. Like any good surgeon, al-Zahrawi selflessly helped countless people beyond his lifetime.

CHAPTER 13:
The Barber Surgeons

Despite the advances of skilled surgeons like al-Zahrawi, going to the doctor was a risky business for a long time.

During the Middle Ages, the barber surgeons were a perfect example of people who **meant well**, but whose medical knowledge was limited.

Why were they called barber surgeons? They started out just cutting hair, but then thought:

Hey! We're good with razors and scissors! Why don't we give **surgery** a try?

Great idea! What could go wrong?

SNIP

The barber surgeons cut off warts and lanced boils.

They could also perform simple dentistry like pulling teeth.

POP

But one of the most common ways to cure many ailments wasn't that great. It was called . . .

Bloodletting!!

Bloodletting involved draining "bad" blood from the body—typically from the forearm or neck—to restore the body back to health. It wasn't a new practice—the Egyptians began doing it in 3000 BCE.

The barber surgeons thought bloodletting would solve all **sorts** of problems, from headaches to indigestion to pneumonia. They used tools with funny-sounding names like **fleams** (blades with handles) and **lancets** (long needles) to carry out this bloody task.

We believed illness is in the blood, so getting rid of blood gets rid of the illness.

Bloodletting wasn't an exact science. Barber surgeons bled patients until they passed out.

Afterward, death (not surprisingly) was a common occurrence.

He would have gotten better if he hadn't **died**!

This didn't stop barber surgeons from trying out new methods to drain blood from people. One such method was

Leeches have **3 jaws and 300 teeth**!

Leeches feed on blood, and for centuries people had used them to suck blood from problem areas.

Sometimes up to 20 leeches might be used.

Despite the yuck factor, leeching was a go-to medical solution for centuries as a cure for many medical issues.

During the leeching heyday, it is estimated that **1 million leeches** were used every year!

In 1855, a boy reported being treated by a doctor with leeches up his nostrils, his lower lip, and his chest and side—all for a **fever**!

And this was one of **many** leechings he had already experienced in his life.

CHAPTER 14: SURGERY becomes EASIER

For centuries, surgery remained at the surface of the skin. Few dared to go **inside** the body. Finding solutions to some key problems allowed surgeons to develop more advanced surgery.

Blood from injuries poured into body cavities, making it difficult to perform surgery. Then people figured out how to tie off blood vessels.

No one really knew about the dangers of germs. Better hygiene reduced the risk of infection from surgery.

And pain was an obstacle. Once effective anesthetics became common, surgeons could work more slowly and carefully.

After these advances, surgeons could go under the skin to fix internal problems.

And there were some surgeons who made great advances in surgery.

One of the most famous surgeons of all time was

ROBERT LISTON

Liston was a skilled surgeon who could confidently amputate a leg in under 30 seconds. It might have been messy and bloody, but he got the job done fast so that his patients didn't suffer long. And his survival rate was better than most surgeons too.

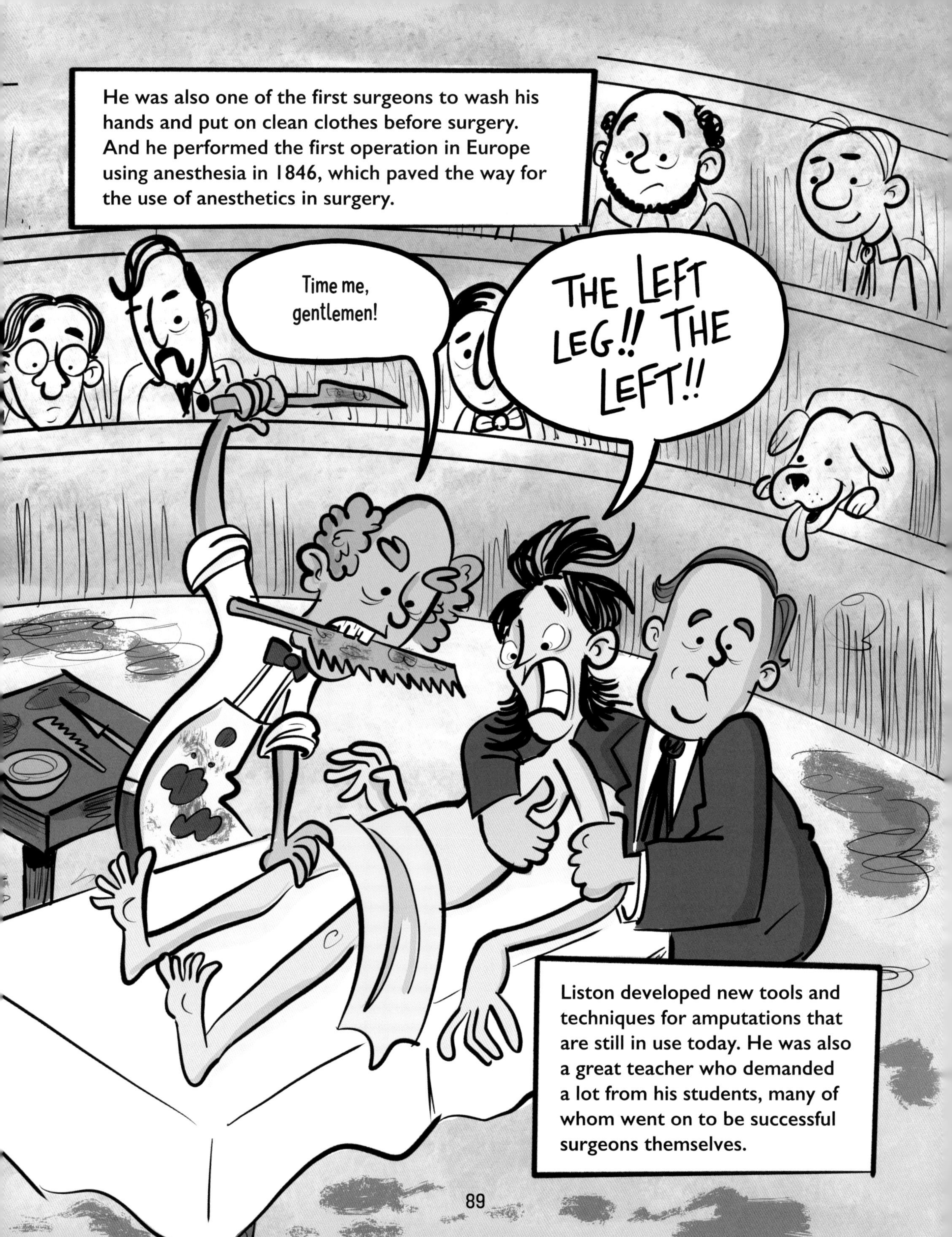
He was also one of the first surgeons to wash his hands and put on clean clothes before surgery. And he performed the first operation in Europe using anesthesia in 1846, which paved the way for the use of anesthetics in surgery.
Time me, gentlemen!
THE LEFT LEG!! THE LEFT!!
Liston developed new tools and techniques for amputations that are still in use today. He was also a great teacher who demanded a lot from his students, many of whom went on to be successful surgeons themselves.

DANIEL HALE WILLIAMS

Williams founded Provident Hospital in Chicago in 1891. It was the first hospital run by Black surgeons.

Williams and the other doctors treated both Black patients and white patients at a time when medicine was still segregated.

One night in 1893, a man named James Cornish was brought to the hospital.

My word! What happened?!

He was **stabbed** in the chest!

Let's take him right to the operating room!

He was stabbed between **two ribs**!

His **heart** might be damaged!

I'll cut a trapdoor between the ribs to see what's going on!

Williams saw there was a cut in the pericardium (the sac of tissue that protects the heart) and set out to repair it.

I'll have to do it without cutting into the heart!

Cornish's heart beat steadily as Williams set out to repair the wound.

I'll hold the edges of the gash with forceps and sew it together!

Williams's surgery was a success. Cornish left the hospital 51 days later and made a full recovery.

Try to avoid any more knives!

Williams continued to perform heart surgeries and train future surgeons—both Black and white—how to do them successfully.

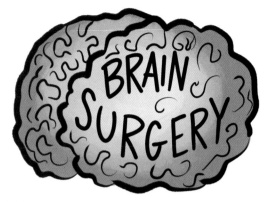

Although people had been trepanning for thousands of years, no one was operating directly on the brain.

In the 14th century, people began to really study anatomy to see how the body worked.

For years, the brain remained a mystery.

There's no moving parts!

It's hard to get to because of the skull!

It's soft and squishy!

By the 17th century, through dissection and examining brain tissue with microscopes, scientists had an even better understanding of how the brain worked.

Starting in the 16th century, scientists began to identify which part of the brain caused strokes and muscular disorders.

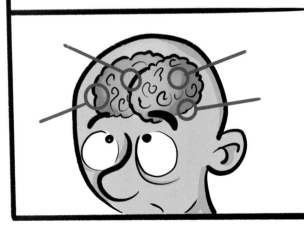

Many doctors were still afraid to operate on the brain.

Too risky!

But some brave surgeons were willing to give it a try.

One day in Scotland in 1879 a doctor named

WILLIAM MACEWEN

performed the first successful

brain tumor surgery.

A fourteen-year-old named Barbara Watson came to Macewen with swelling over her left eye.

She was also having seizures in her face and one of her arms.

Macewen knew she had a brain tumor. Brain surgery was still rare in 1879, but Macewen had done his research.

Macewen sedated the girl and removed a part of her skull.

Hmm ... seizures ... I know **exactly** where the tumor is!

Let's get this thing **out**!

Macewen cut out the tumor, repaired the hole, and Watson made a full recovery.

I can remember everything! Even the taste of (ugh) broccoli!

It was a landmark achievement in medicine! Brain surgery became safer and more effective after Macewen proved it could be done.

In the 1930s in New England, two doctors made a huge contribution to the knowledge of brain surgery:

HARVEY CUSHING (neurosurgeon) AND **LOUISE EISENHARDT** (neuropathologist)

Cushing was a brain surgeon and started collecting specimens of various tumors and damaged brains so that other surgeons could learn from them.

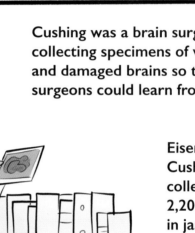

Eisenhardt helped Cushing organize his collection of more than 2,200 brain specimens in jars and on slides.

In the process they became brain experts, helping surgeons identify tumors and how to remove them.

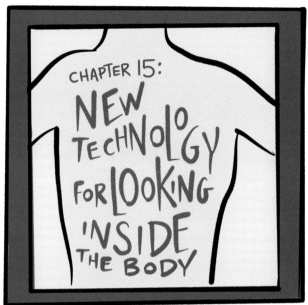

CHAPTER 15: NEW TECHNOLOGY FOR LOOKING INSIDE THE BODY

Many injuries are visible just by looking at the patient.

I think you might have a broken arm.

But for a long time if you had internal injuries, doctors had no choice but to open up the body to see what was wrong.

Many doctors wouldn't even try, because the risk of death or infection was high when surgeons cut open the skin. Many patients would live longer if the doctor left them alone.

Let's cut him open and see what the trouble is!

But starting in the late 1800s, people invented machines that allowed surgeons to peer inside the body without even touching it. And they led to the next important step in surgery.

One day in 1895 a physicist named Wilhelm Roentgen was playing around in his lab in Germany.

He was working with cathode ray tubes, which give off a fluorescent glow when a current passes through a gas inside.

He encased a tube in thick black cardboard, dimmed the lights, and sat back to see what happened.

To his surprise, even though the tube was completely covered, a nearby screen lit up!

It must be some sort of **radiation**!

Roetgen had discovered a type of light that could go through solid objects.

I'll call them **X-rays**.

"X" stands for the **UNKNOWN!**

Roentgen thought X-rays might allow him to see through people too. One of the first things he X-rayed was his wife's hand.

I can see all the bones inside!

Doctors and surgeons everywhere loved this new discovery because it allowed them to locate foreign objects without opening the patient up . . .

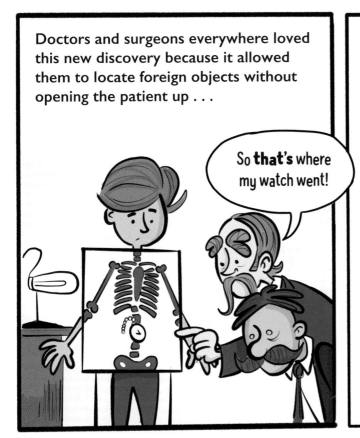

So **that's** where my watch went!

. . . or figure out **exactly** where a bone was broken. No more guessing!

Roentgen received a lot of awards for the discovery of X-rays but was a humble man who didn't like attention.

In 1901, I was awarded the first Nobel Prize for physics, but I donated the prize money to scientific research.

I also refused to patent the X-ray so that everyone could benefit from it.

Not only was he smart, he was also generous!

There are two more recent technologies that doctors use to get an even better picture of your insides.

CAT Scans

A **CAT scan**, also known as a **CT scan**, uses X-rays and computer technology to create detailed images of the inside of the body.

A patient lies on a table that moves through a machine that captures multiple X-ray images of the body from different angles.

The images are then combined by a computer to create a 3D image of the body, allowing doctors to see the internal structures of organs and tissues in great detail.

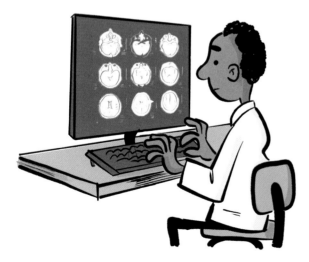

The images produced by a CAT scan provide doctors with information about what's wrong and how to proceed.

Looks like you're fine! Just wear a helmet when you snowboard!

AND MRIS

Doctors use an **MRI**, or Magnetic Resonance Imaging, to examine injuries to internal organs or joints.

The MRI has a powerful magnet that temporarily disrupts the organization of your body's atoms.

As your body's atoms jiggle around, the machine takes lots of pictures quickly. They are put together by a computer to create a detailed 3D image of your insides.

An MRI can not only show doctors what your organs and tissues look like, but it can also show how they're working.

CAT scans and MRIs give doctors valuable information about how to proceed with surgery—or even if the patient needs it!

All clear!

WHAT'S NEXT: ROBOT SURGERY

Imagine if you could have an operation anywhere in the world. Like a battlefield. Or Antarctica. Or even a space station!

Telesurgery might provide the solution. With telesurgery, surgeons can take their skills across the world. All they need is robotics and a high-speed internet connection.

This is Dr. Singh. She's from the (not-too-distant) future!

I'm going to perform surgery on a patient on a space station from a hospital in Cleveland.

I receive data over the internet about the patient. I look through a video monitor and direct the robot on the space station using hand controls.

The patient is in an operating room on the space station with a robot and a few attendants.

The robot arms have greater dexterity and accuracy than my hands. I'll finish the surgery in no time flat and with few complications.

"Telesurgery brings surgery to places where good medical care is scarce, like impoverished nations or places that are remote."

"And people everywhere would have access to specialized surgeries because surgeons wouldn't have to travel long distances to use their skills."

Chuck Hicks - World's only pinky toenail surgeon

Telesurgery still faces some obstacles. It requires expensive equipment at two locations.

Also, current internet bandwidth is not able to quickly transmit large quantities of information over extremely long distances.

However, it's possible in your lifetime that you'll go under the knife and there won't be a surgeon present!

ERIC RETURNS FROM THE HOSPITAL

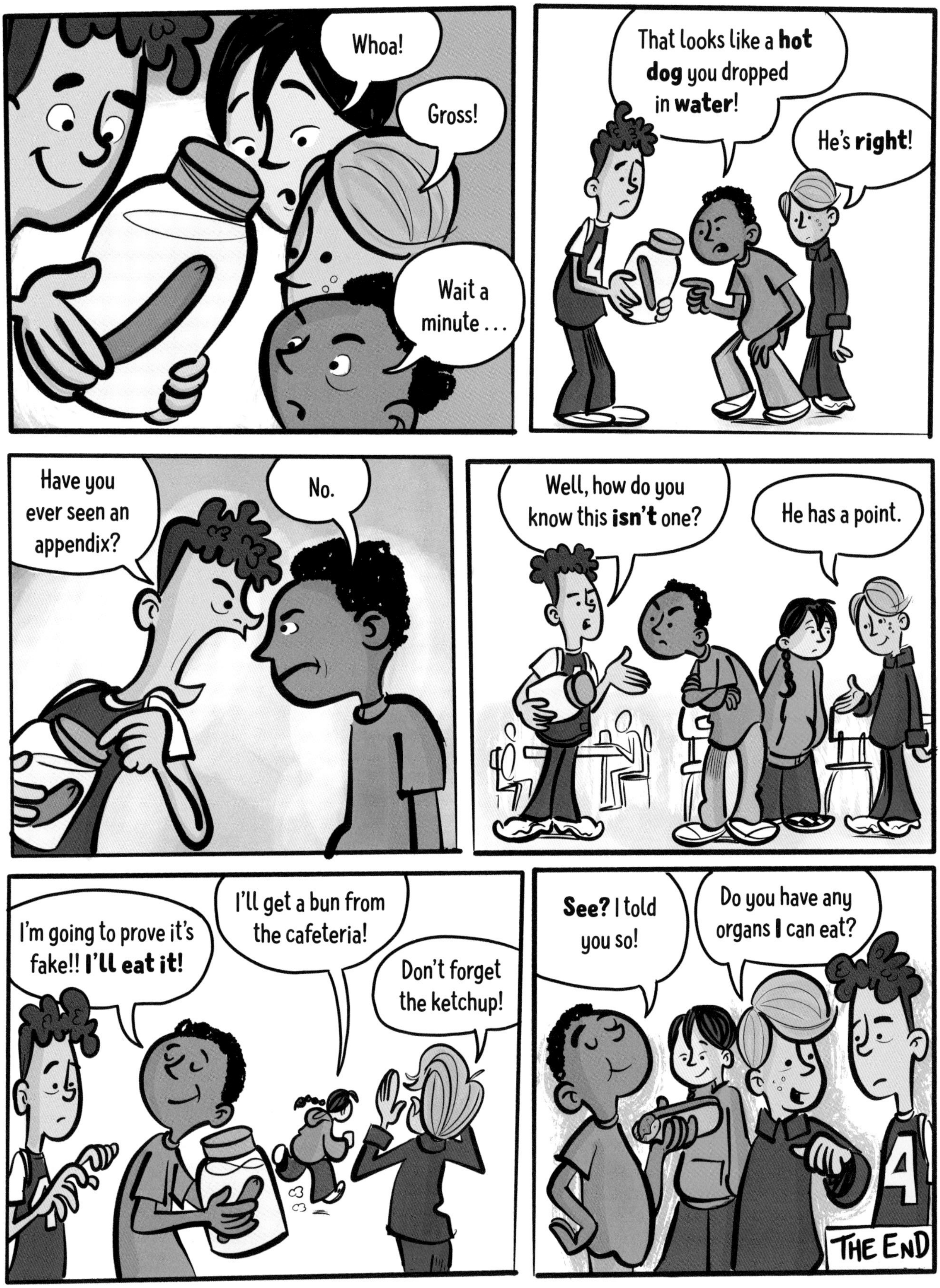
Whoa!
Gross!
Wait a minute . . .
That looks like a **hot dog** you dropped in **water**!
He's **right**!
Have you ever seen an appendix?
No.
Well, how do you know this **isn't** one?
He has a point.
I'm going to prove it's fake!! **I'll eat it!**
I'll get a bun from the cafeteria!
Don't forget the ketchup!
See? I told you so!
Do you have any organs **I** can eat?
THE END

Still Curious?

There's more!

Create a Medical History Comic!

Pick **me**!
You're not famous!

First Aid You Can Do Yourself!

Make Your Own First Aid Kit!

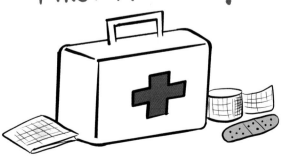

RESEARCHING A FAMOUS DOCTOR

Now that you've read about famous doctors, you might like to do your own research on a famous doctor who isn't covered here. There are **a lot** to choose from.

> I'd like to learn more about important women doctors.

First, go to the internet and search for a doctor.

> I'm going to search for "important women doctors."

Check out several sources to gather information. Make sure they are reliable sources!

> Hmm . . . Patricia Bath worked on blindness prevention and treatment. That's cool.

> The National Institutes of Health looks good. So does this one from the University of Toronto.

Collect basic biographical data.

> She was born in 1942 and went to medical school at Howard University.

NOW IT'S TIME TO DIG IN! WHAT MAKES THEM AN IMPORTANT DOCTOR?

Look for the major accomplishments of your doctor. How did they help people with medical problems?

In 1976 Dr. Bath cofounded the American Institute for the Prevention of Blindness.

Eyesight is a basic human right!

Add any other facts that are both important and interesting.

Bath noticed that Black people were twice as likely as white people to go blind.

She started **community programs** to provide screening and eye care for underserved communities.

Congratulations! You are now an expert on your doctor. Be sure to share your knowledge with everyone (or at least your friends and family). Your doctor deserves the recognition!

Great job, sweetie!

HOW I DRAW FAMOUS PEOPLE

For this book I had to draw **a lot** of famous doctors. The first thing I did was look for pictures of them, and if I found one that was interesting, that was the one I chose.

Here is a great picture of William Morton from the "Pain" section that I used for reference. Interesting-looking fellow, isn't he?

I look for the overall shape of their head. Morton's looks like a diamond, and I'll use this basic shape for the head outline.

Now it's time to work on the face. I draw an oval for the head using the shape as a guide. Then, I draw a cross in the middle of the head. This is where the eyes and nose will go.

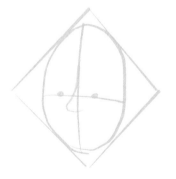

Then I draw the face and hair. I like to pick a few features to really exaggerate. Does it look exactly like Morton? No, but I'm creating an interesting design, not an exact likeness.

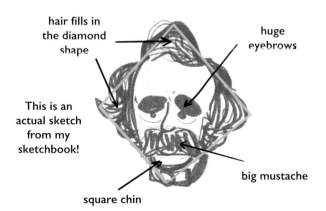

hair fills in the diamond shape

huge eyebrows

This is an actual sketch from my sketchbook!

big mustache

square chin

Then I try a bunch of different expressions so that I **really** get to know my new character.

I always sketch people from the left. I don't know why.

How I draw eyes closed

still using the diamond shape

Eyebrows are the key to good expressions

Mustaches are fun!

Hair shows anger too!

Laughter. The same expression works for shouting with a few tweaks. You'll see it a lot in the book.

Then I add the rest of the body and the clothes. I couldn't find a picture of Morton from head to toe, so I just looked for clothing from the time period to finish off his outfit. (I have some books of clothing styles over time, and there's always the internet.) Since I'm only going to draw him a couple of times, I don't need to look for changes of clothing.

Here's the version of Morton I'm going to use. I took the collar from the picture I found and made up the rest.

Then I'll draw him in a few different poses, so I understand the character and make sure that my design works. I don't want the page layouts to be the first time I draw him so I practice first. Sometimes I get lucky and when I'm sketching, I find a drawing I can use! Can you find one of these in the book?

It's Time to Create Your COMIC!!

Step 1:

Plan your script. Do this panel by panel. Don't use too many words! Save room for the artwork.

> Panel 1: Frederick Banting discovered insulin in 1921.

> Panel 2: It originally came from cows! Udderly amazing!

(Puns are **always** good.)

Step 2:

Once you have your script done, plan out your images.

> I'll draw Banting with a cow!

Step 3.

Now it's time to create! All you need is paper and something to draw with.

> You can use anything to create comics. Experiment!

Step 4:

Divide your paper into three rows. Divide the rows into panels. Six is a good number, but you can use as many or as few as you want.

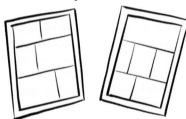

Step 5:

Important! Add your words before you draw so that you have enough room for the text. If you don't, divide the text into two panels.

> Not enough room for drawings.

Step 6:

You already have your character design for your doctor, but you'll need to look up other stuff too.

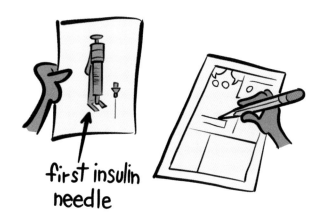

first insulin needle

Step 7:

You also might want to search for what a doctor's office or a hospital looked like back then.

That's a lot of bottles and tubes!

Step 8:

Color your work if you want to. Markers tend to bleed. Use crayons or colored pencils instead.

Step 9:

You did it! Share your finished work with your friends, family, and teachers. Hopefully they will learn something new!

I didn't know that!

BASIC FIRST AID YOU CAN

You're probably used to getting help from adults when you have a medical problem. But sometimes adults aren't around. Here are some simple things you can do for yourself.

BLOODY NOSE

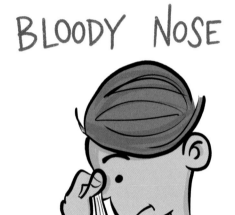

Don't tilt your head back! Blood might go down your throat.

– Lean slightly forward and use a towel or tissue to pinch your nose right above the nostrils.
– Wait 10–15 minutes for the nosebleed to stop.

When to get help: If the bleeding doesn't stop after 30 minutes or it appears that the nose might be broken.

MINOR BURNS

Don't use ice! It can damage the skin.

– Run the burn under cold water or use a towel soaked in cold water.
– Clean the burn with soap and water. Apply a light layer of antibiotic ointment.

When to get help: If the burn is larger than your palm, or if it's on your face, ears, hands, or feet.

DO YOURSELF!!

Can I perform brain surgery on my own?

Not a good idea.

CUTS AND SCRAPES

– Apply direct pressure with gauze for 10 minutes.
– Clean the wound with soap and water for 5 minutes.
– Dab on antibiotic ointment and apply a bandage.
– If it bleeds through the bandage, raise the wound above the heart to stop the bleeding.

When to get help:
– If the cut won't stop bleeding within 15 minutes.
– If it appears there's some object in the cut.
– If you can see muscle or bone.

TWISTED ANKLE

Follow the RICE method:
– **Rest** the ankle. Keep weight off of it.
– **Ice** the ankle with ice or an ice pack for 10–20 minutes, 3 or more times a day.
– **Compression**—wrap the ankle with an elastic bandage to help decrease swelling, but don't wrap too tightly!
– **Elevate** your ankle above your heart to reduce swelling.

When to get help: If you can't put any pressure on your foot or if it looks **really** bad.

IMPORTANT!

Find an adult or call 9-1-1 if the injury is one you can't handle on your own.

How To Make A BASIC FIRST AID KIT

You should always have a basic first aid kit at home. Here's what to put in:

2 compress dressings

25 assorted adhesive bandages

adhesive cloth tape

5 antibiotic ointment packets

5 antiseptic wipe packets

2 packets of aspirin

1 instant cold compress

2 pairs of nonlatex gloves

2 hydrocortisone ointment packets

3 in. gauze roll bandages

roller bandage

tweezers

emergency first aid instructions

any emergency medications for family members (like for allergic reactions)

Further Reading

Books For Kids

Arnold, Nick. *Do No Harm: A Painful History of Medicine.* Wellbeck Children's Limited, 2021.

History for Kids: Medical Revolution: Medical Inventions 1700s to Present. Dinobibi Publishing, 2019.

Messner, Kate. *History Smashers: Plagues and Pandemics.* New York: Random House BFYR, 2021.

Parker, Steve. *Medicine: The Definitive Illustrated History.* New York: DK Publishing, 2016.

Wagner, Kristie. *Human Anatomy for Kids: A Junior Scientist's Guide to How We Move, Breathe, and Grow.* Emeryville, CA: Rockridge Press, 2021.

Wicks, Maris. *Human Body Theater: A Nonfiction Revue.* New York: First Second, 2015.

Books on First Aid

Boelts, Maribeth. *Kids to the Rescue!: First Aid Techniques for Kids.* Seattle, WA: Parenting Press, 2003.

Websites

History Channel: history.com. Do a search for "medicine" and you'll find articles.

National Library of Medicine Profiles in Science: profiles.nlm.nih.gov.

Nemours KidsHealth: kidshealth.org.

Smithsonian Magazine Mind & Body section: smithsonianmag.com/category/mind-body. You can also do a search for "medicine" here and find some really interesting articles!

For Adults (Like Teachers and Parents)

Kang, Lydia, and Nate Pedersen. *Quackery: A Brief History of the Worst Ways to Cure Everything.* New York: Workman Publishing, 2017.

McElroy, Justin, and Dr. Sydney McElroy. *Sawbones: The Horrifying, Hilarious Road to Modern Medicine.* Weldon Owen, 2018.

Mukherjee, Siddhartha. *The Emperor of All Maladies: A Biography of Cancer.* New York, Scribner, 2011.

Rutkow, Ira M. *Empire of the Scalpel: The History of Surgery.* New York: Scribner, 2022.

Index

Acknowledgments

Once again, there were a lot of people who helped make this book happen.

My editor, Harold Underdown, took a basic idea and helped me work through several concepts before we settled on this one. He understood the type of work I wanted to create and provided many helpful suggestions along the way.

My agent, Janna Morishima, provided support behind the scenes and was a frequent cheerleader. I'm happy to have her as a believer in my work.

I also would like to thank Ray, Symon, Melia, Kerry, Chelsea, and everyone else at Kane Press who made this book look great and put up with my lack of attention to detail.

There were a handful of doctors who were eager to help fact-check and answer questions about whether what I was doing made any sense. Ansley Splinter, Darren Berman, and Andrew Yates were valuable medical resources.

I would like to thank Renee Harleston of Writing Diversely for her suggestions, and for Anthony Bowersock for fact-checking with a doctor's thoroughness. Copyeditors Nancy Seitz, Suzanne Lander, and Sarah Thomson made sure that everything sounded as good as it could.

I continue to have the best critique group in the world: Sarah Giles, Cesar Lador, Ken Rolston, and Lana Le.

Dave Plunkett was my drawing buddy for several years. He's probably disappointed there are no dragons in this book, but he was always better at drawing them than I was.

I want to thank all of the people who bought and enjoyed my first books and especially those who sent pictures of their kids reading it. That kept my spirits up in the midst of creating this one.

To my parents for their continued support in all I do.

To Julie, Jack, and Lily who let me work on my book. I hope you are proud of what I did.

To all of the physicians I visited while working on this book for keeping me healthy.

And finally to all the great musicians who provided the soundtrack for me while I worked.

About the Author

David grew up in Columbus, Ohio surrounded by stacks of *MAD Magazines*, Calvin and Hobbes collections, and Walt Disney comics. He spent most of his free time learning about sable hair brushes, non-repro blue pencils, and Bristol board so he could pursue a career drawing a comic strip.

However, he went to The Ohio State University instead to pursue a degree in education. But he never gave up on the dream! He drew a daily strip in *The Lantern* (The Ohio State University's school newspaper) for most of his college years. After receiving a teaching degree and spending a few years in the classroom, the itch to create comics resurfaced. He headed back to the drawing board (literally) to create educational comics, selling them on the Teachers Pay Teachers marketplace. Educators from around the world have enthusiastically embraced his comics as an effective way to approach difficult language arts concepts, especially to reluctant readers and English language learners.

His first nonfiction graphic novel, *Pizza, Pickles, and Apple Pie: The Stories Behind the Foods We Love,* was released in 2023.